Frommer's®

MEMORABLE WALKS IN
CHICAGO

4th Edition

Elizabeth Canning Blackwell & Todd A. Savage

WILEY

Wiley Publishing, Inc.

Published by:

WILEY PUBLISHING, INC.

909 Third Ave.
New York, NY 10022

ISBN 0-7645-6742-X
ISSN 1096-6552

Editor: Stephen Bassman
Production Editor: Heather Wilcox
Photo Editor: Richard Fox
Cartographer: John Decamillis
Production by Wiley Indianapolis Composition Services

For information on our other products and services or to obtain technical support, please contact our Customer Care Department within the
U.S. at 800-762-2974, outside the U.S. at 317-572-3993 or fax
317-572-4002.

Wiley also publishes its books in a variety of electronic formats. Some
content that appears in print may not be available in electronic formats.

Manufactured in the United States of America

5   4   3   2   1

Contents

LIST OF MAPS

The Walking Tours

• • • • • • • • • • • • • • • •

About the Authors

Elizabeth Canning Blackwell began life on the East Coast, but 4 years at Northwestern University transformed her into a Midwesterner. She has worked as a writer and editor at Encyclopedia Britannica, Northwestern University Medical School, and *North Shore,* a lifestyle magazine for the Chicago suburbs. She also has written for national magazines on everything from planning the perfect wedding to fighting a duel. She lives in Chicago with her husband.

Todd A. Savage has lived in the Chicago area on and off for more than a decade. He has written about the city for a variety of local publications, including the *Chicago Reader,* the *Chicago Tribune,* and *Chicago* magazine, as well as national magazines such as *Metropolis* and *Travel & Leisure.*

An Invitation to the Reader

In researching this book, we discovered many wonderful places—hotels, restaurants, shops, and more. We're sure you'll find others. Please tell us about them, so we can share the information with your fellow travelers in upcoming editions. If you were disappointed with a recommendation, we'd love to know that, too. Please write to:

Frommer's Memorable Walks in Chicago, 4th Edition
Wiley Publishing, Inc.
909 Third Ave. • New York, NY 10022

An Additional Note

Please be advised that travel information is subject to change at any time—and this is especially true of prices. We therefore suggest that you write or call ahead for confirmation when making your travel plans. The authors, editors, and publisher cannot be held responsible for the experiences of readers while traveling. Your safety is important to us, however, so we encourage you to stay alert and be aware of your surroundings. Keep a close eye on cameras, purses, and wallets, all favorite targets of thieves and pickpockets.

FROMMERS.COM

Now that you have the guidebook to a great trip, visit our website at **www.frommers.com** for travel information on nearly 2,500 destinations. With features updated regularly, we give you instant access to the most current trip-planning information available. At Frommers.com, you'll also find the best prices on airfares, accommodations, and car rentals—and you can even book travel online through our travel booking partners. At Frommers.com, you'll also find the following:

- Online updates to our most popular guidebooks
- Vacation sweepstakes and contest giveaways
- Newsletter highlighting the hottest travel trends
- Online travel message boards with featured travel discussions

Introducing Chicago

There are really only two big cities in America: New York and Chicago. Big cities require tall buildings, dense downtown areas, street life, and sprawling neighborhoods radiating out from the center—neighborhoods that project urban, not suburban, flavor. As big American cities go, New York tops the list. Chicago has never suggested that it might surpass the great metropolis of the East. Indeed, Chicago has long dubbed itself the "Second City." But the boosters here—who gave Chicago another of its many nicknames, the "Windy City"—aren't just blowing hot air when they boast about the quality of life in the "City by the Lake."

Civic pride runs high in Chicago; it always has. When the rest of the world could only imagine Chicago as a haven for crooks and corrupt politicians, as a "jungle" of slaughterhouses and meat-packers, Chicagoans went about their worldly affairs—one of which involved building the most architecturally sophisticated city in the world. In a head-on race with New York, architectural innovation against architectural innovation, Chicago wins hands down.

For years, Chicago has had the most successful convention trade in the country. Recently, more and more "destination" travelers, international and domestic, have been drawn to the city. They're coming to have a good time. Bed for bed, you'd be hard pressed to find a city with a better infrastructure of fine hotels. And you don't have to be rich to stay in one—at least if you come on the weekends, when rates often drop, and packages can include amenities from breakfast and free parking to tickets for a local show. As for the food, Chicago's reputation as a place where you'd better stick to steak is long gone. You still might not be able to find better steaks, chops, and ribs anywhere else in America, but in modern culinary terms, this town has grown up. Its restaurants can go toe to toe with the best of them . . . anywhere!

CHICAGO'S ROOTS

The city you see before you has its modern roots in the early 19th century; Chicago is a relatively recent phenomenon, even in the context of the historical youth of the United States. Indeed, use of the word "phenomenon" is not an exaggeration. In 1840, Chicago had a population of barely 5,000; by 1880 the number had increased a hundredfold, totaling 500,000. Chicago's growth was a yardstick against which the American Republic could measure the realization of its Manifest Destiny, the inexorable spread of its authority and settlements from coast to coast.

European explorers recognized the significance of the location that is now Chicago as early as 1673. In that year, Native Americans led Jacques Marquette and Louis Jolliet, who had labored assiduously to expand the French Empire throughout North America, to a portage trail. It ran between two nearby, disconnected rivers that linked ancient trade routes of the Mississippi Valley to those along Lake Michigan and beyond. The passage created, in effect, an inland waterway between the Atlantic Ocean and the Gulf of Mexico. Chicago lay at the perfect intersection of those two water routes, at the mouth of the river on the eastern end of the portage, which emptied into Lake Michigan.

Not until 1803, two decades after the War of Independence ended, did the fledgling Republic establish its military presence: A frontier fort occupied the site where the Michigan Avenue Bridge today crosses the Chicago River. But tensions between Native Americans and white settlers grew. Fort Dearborn was destroyed, and its inhabitants were massacred during a raid in 1812. Four years later, the fort was

The Tours at a Glance

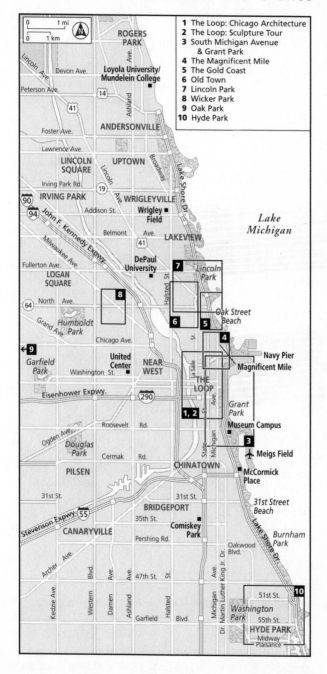

1 The Loop: Chicago Architecture
2 The Loop: Sculpture Tour
3 South Michigan Avenue
   & Grant Park
4 The Magnificent Mile
5 The Gold Coast
6 Old Town
7 Lincoln Park
8 Wicker Park
9 Oak Park
10 Hyde Park

A Key to Chicago's Architecture

When exploring a city with Chicago's architectural legacy, it makes sense to familiarize yourself with some of the architectural and building styles you'll encounter. Here are my picks for the key terms:

Chicago School of Architecture: The steel-frame construction of the late 19th century led to this homegrown style, characterized by three-part windows with large central panes flanked by smaller double-hung sash windows, a minimal use of ornamentation, and masonry exteriors, often terra-cotta, that emphasized a building's steel frame. Examples are the Reliance Building and Carson Pirie Scott store. After World War II, a **Second School of Chicago Architecture** developed as Mies van der Rohe and other modernists pioneered the boxy steel-and-glass skyscrapers of the International Style, such as the Inland Steel Building, IBM Building, and Federal Plaza.

Prairie School: Chicago's claim to architectural fame rests firmly with this purely American style developed in the late 19th and early 20th centuries by Frank Lloyd Wright and his contemporaries. It is distinguished by horizontal lines, flat brick or stucco walls, windows with geometric ornamentation, and hip roofs with wide overhanging eaves.

Queen Anne: This style, popular in the 1880s and 1890s, is found nearly everywhere in the United States and is common in many Chicago neighborhoods. Buildings have asymmetrical shapes with bays and turrets, spacious porches, shingle and clapboard surfaces, prominent rooflines, and elegant but simple ornaments like stained glass.

rebuilt. In 1833, with a population of slightly more than 300 inhabitants, the town of Chicago was officially incorporated.

The town originated as a transportation and shipping hub for pioneers and for materials headed west, in exchange for grain and livestock going east. It soon developed into a major

Romanesque Revival: A man's home is literally his castle if it was designed in this powerful architectural style. The forms were taken from the 11th- and 12th-century architecture of France and Spain but were re-interpreted and revived in the 1880s through the work of Boston architect H. H. Richardson (the style is also known as Richardsonian). In Chicago, look for heavy, rough-cut stone walls; round arches; deeply recessed windows; and bays and turrets on houses and commercial buildings.

Second Empire (also **beaux arts** or **French Empire**): Turning to the Italian Renaissance, Louis IV, and Napoléon III for inspiration, this classical style sought to bring dignity and strength to public buildings. Distinguishing features of this style of the 1860s and 1870s are sloping mansard roofs, prominent cornices, and detailed stonework around doors and windows. It was popular in Chicago following the Great Fire, yet few examples survive today.

Stick: This late-19th-century style, often found in homes in Chicago, is noted for its use of wood construction, notably decorative planks (thus, the name) outlining the structure's wood frame, and decorative wooden details.

Sullivanesque: The style of influential Chicago architect Louis Sullivan, creator of the Auditorium Building and Carson Pirie Scott department store, is identified by masonry walls and terra-cotta ornamentation with lush organic forms and geometric patterns.

industrial and manufacturing center in its own right. Regional deposits of coal and iron ore led to the establishment of steel mills and factories that produced heavy machinery. But playing the role of middleman between East and West never ceased to be a major factor in Chicago's economy. It's no coincidence

Chicago & Vicinity

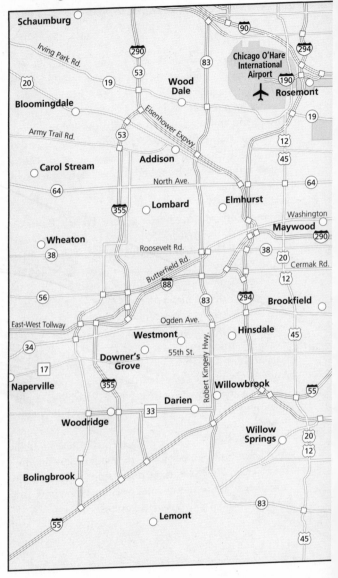

that the mail-order giants of the American retail trade, like Sears, Roebuck & Company and Montgomery Ward, grew up and retained their headquarters in Chicago. For many decades, nearly every train originating on either coast (and any point in

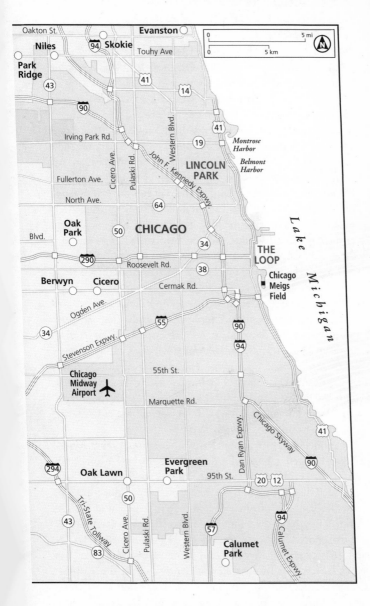

between, for that matter) passed through Chicago. With connections like that, it didn't take the city long to become the hub of industry, manufacturing, commerce, and finance for the core of the country.

THE GREAT FIRE

Who, then, could have anticipated that the vibrant, rough-and-ready frontier metropolis of the heartland would be nearly struck from the map in two short days? On the southwest side of the city, in the barn where Mrs. O'Leary's fabled cow was thought to have resided, a fire began on the evening of October 8, 1871. The flames, fed by acres of wooden homes and roadway planking, quickly spread north, consuming all of downtown before leaping the Chicago River and leveling residential neighborhoods as far north as present-day Fullerton Avenue. By October 10, with the help of explosives, the flames moving south were checked. Rainfall finally quenched the northside fires, ending the long drought that had made tinder of the city's wooden structures just before the flames spread to the grassy plains of the surrounding prairie.

More than 250 residents lost their lives. Eighteen thousand buildings were reduced to ashes, leaving 90,000 people homeless. Damage was assessed at $200 million. An area covering 4 square miles, including the business district, was completely destroyed. Two major resources remained unscathed, however. The first, inherently immutable, was Chicago's strategic location; the second, of more immediate significance, was the city's infrastructure of railroads, manufacturing plants, grain warehouses, and lumberyards, which had been miraculously spared. Most of those facilities were on the city's southern rim, beyond the circle of the fire.

With the aid of national and international relief funds, Chicago staged a remarkable comeback. By 1873, the city's downtown business district had already been rebuilt. The Great Fire had spurred an unprecedented renaissance in construction and architecture. From 1885, when William Le Baron Jenny built the Home Insurance Building (considered the first modern skyscraper) to 1894, 21 buildings between 12 and 16 stories high were erected in downtown Chicago. By 1893, Chicago had recovered sufficiently to host the World's Columbian Exposition, an honor it won over four other contending American cities, including New York.

THE CRADLE OF THE AMERICAN LABOR MOVEMENT

Yankee ingenuity was the driving force behind the initial growth and success of Chicago. The early pioneers followed the westward migration, leaving ancestral homes in the Northeast. But the real population explosion in Chicago was a by-product of 19th-century mass migration from Europe. By 1890, the foreign-born and their children made up three-quarters of Chicago's population. The immigrants made the factories run, providing the "big shoulders" upon which Chicago's industrial and merchant princes made great fortunes.

From the 1870s through the 1890s, most of the labor battles in the United States—for shorter hours, higher wages, and better working conditions—centered in the mills and factories of Chicago. Two legendary struggles, the Pullman Strike and the issues leading up to the so-called Haymarket Riot, will live forever in the annals of American labor as high-water marks in the worker's quest for fairness and justice on the job. May Day, as an international day commemorating workers, originated on May 1, 1886, in a Chicago parade calling for the 8-hour work day.

POLITICS, GANGSTERS & RACE

By virtue of its location, Chicago also developed into a power-house on the national political scene. Between 1860 and 1996, Chicago played host to 14 Republican and 11 Democratic presidential nominating conventions. The first Chicago convention gave the nation one of its most admired leaders, Abraham Lincoln. Riots between Chicago police and anti-Vietnam War demonstrators accompanied the 1968 Democratic convention, which nominated Hubert Humphrey.

No image of this city is more enduring, especially beyond our national borders, than that of Chicago as a haven for tommy gun–toting gangsters and their corrupt allies (politicians, judges, cops, and journalists) during Prohibition. While by no means completely false, this image was never more than a caricature, and little trace of those wild days remains apparent in Chicago today. It's not that organized crime has disappeared, nor that political corruption has been eliminated, but the problems of Chicago are not those of its mythic past. Most of Chicago's difficulties today are those that plague every American city: crime, population flight, and declining fiscal resources, especially in the areas of social services, public transit, and education. As in other American cities, racial tensions often aggravate these problems.

More than most large American cities, Chicago has managed to keep up appearances. The city, especially in the areas covered by these walking tours, seems amazingly peaceful and clean—almost polished in places. A flurry of new construction downtown and in many neighborhoods is adding to Chicago's luster. Chicagoans demonstrate pride that their city remains a very livable place. Their view is often shared by visitors who are discovering the city's charms for the first time or are returning to deepen their relationship with this most American of American cities.

The Loop:
Chicago
Architecture

Start: Sears Tower, 233 S. Wacker Dr., at West Jackson Boulevard.

Public Transportation: Take the Brown, Green, Purple, or Orange line to the Quincy/Wells station. You can also catch a bus from various downtown locations; nos. 1, 7, 151, and 156 all pass near the Sears Tower.

Finish: Harold Washington Library Center, 400 S. State St., at Congress Parkway.

Time: 2 to 3 hours.

Best Times: Weekends during daylight hours, especially Saturdays, when most buildings are open and sidewalk and street traffic are minimal. Weekdays are next best, or even preferable, if you like your cityscapes against a backdrop of human hustle and bustle.

Worst Time: Night, for security and because you can't see well enough to appreciate architectural details.

Downtown Chicago has two poles, north and south of the Chicago River. The old downtown, to the south, is known as the Loop, so called because much of it lies within a large area enclosed by a system of elevated train tracks. The Loop and its immediate environs contain the city's principal financial, cultural, and government centers. Across the Michigan Avenue Bridge, running north along the Magnificent Mile, is the high-rent district of downtown Chicago. It holds the city's newest and most luxurious hotels, vertical malls, and specialty shops, and its most desirable office space (see Walking Tour 4, "The Magnificent Mile"). Still, when city residents mention "downtown," they probably mean the densely packed canyon of buildings in the Loop, whose most venerable structures rose in a burst of reconstruction following the Great Fire of 1871.

Chicago owes its reputation as an architectural mecca to that tragic conflagration, which virtually leveled the town. Since that time, Chicago has been a haven to architects of many visions, who have transformed the Loop into an open-air showroom of architectural style and innovation. It encompasses the engineering of the first skyscrapers; the sprawling, purely functional emporia where merchant princes displayed their acres of commodities; and the fanciful excesses of ornamentation and design associated early on with Louis Sullivan and Frank Lloyd Wright, and more recently with Helmut Jahn and Philip Johnson. For these architects, the ideals of beauty and utility were inseparable.

• • • • • • • • • • • • • • • •

Our walk proceeds from the south end of Wacker Drive, follows the river as it bends toward Lake Michigan, and then plunges south into the core of the Loop, as we zigzag block by block among the neighborhood's most representative architectural oddities and treasures.

Begin at the:

1. **Sears Tower.** At 1,454 feet, it is the nation's tallest building. The world title is a different matter: In 1998, the twin Petronas Towers in Kuala Lumpur surpassed the Sears Tower, largely on the strength of their decorative

The Loop: Chicago Architecture

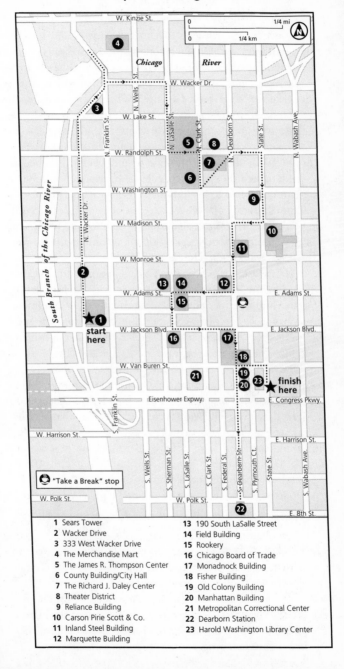

1 Sears Tower
2 Wacker Drive
3 333 West Wacker Drive
4 The Merchandise Mart
5 The James R. Thompson Center
6 County Building/City Hall
7 The Richard J. Daley Center
8 Theater District
9 Reliance Building
10 Carson Pirie Scott & Co.
11 Inland Steel Building
12 Marquette Building
13 190 South LaSalle Street
14 Field Building
15 Rookery
16 Chicago Board of Trade
17 Monadnock Building
18 Fisher Building
19 Old Colony Building
20 Manhattan Building
21 Metropolitan Correctional Center
22 Dearborn Station
23 Harold Washington Library Center

spires. Chicago's monolith can claim three of four distinctions awarded by the International Council on Tall Buildings and Urban Habitat: world's highest occupied office building, highest rooftop, and highest height to the tip of a spire or antenna (categories essentially created to help the Sears Tower save face). When the Sears Company chose this site for its new corporate headquarters, the decision was controversial. Many city planners saw the Loop as a neighborhood in decline. Since its completion in 1974, the mere presence of the giant skyscraper has stimulated the construction of more than 100 new buildings in Chicago's traditional downtown area. (Sears has since relocated its offices to the suburbs.)

The 110-story megatower was built to accommodate 16,500 office workers, 5,000 of whom originally were Sears employees. The Sears Tower's foundation rests on 114 caissons of concrete and steel sunk to bedrock 65 feet below the building's three subbasements. Architecturally, the building, designed by Bruce Graham of Skidmore, Owings & Merrill, is considered more a triumph of engineering than design. Seen from a distance, its unique, imposing profile dominates the Chicago skyline from practically every point on the compass.

A ride to the building's observation deck on the 103rd floor, reached through an entrance on Jackson, is a popular attraction for visitors and residents alike, especially school-age children on field trips. Tickets are $9.90 for adults and $6.75 for children 3 to 11; the observation deck is open daily from 10am to 8pm (until 10pm May–Sept). For more information, call ☎ 312/875-9696 or visit www.sears-tower.com. Be prepared: The line can stack up, with waits of more than an hour in summer.

When you leave the Sears Tower, walk north on:

2. **Wacker Drive.** The many modern buildings lining the drive may or may not appeal to you, but few cities offer a downtown stroll as pleasant as this one. The proximity of the river and the width of the roadway create an atmosphere of openness, as if you're at the bottom of the urban canyon, rather than among the narrow mule paths of the Loop's interior streets.

Wacker Drive is named for Charles Wacker, a civic-minded brewer and a director of the World's Columbian Exposition of 1893. He lobbied tirelessly for a plan to replace the old South Water Street Market, once the principal feature along the riverbank, with this double-level thoroughfare.

As you walk north, you will see on your left the "Merc," or **Chicago Mercantile Exchange Center,** at no. 30 South. It houses one of the great trading chambers for Midwestern commodities. The **Civic Opera Building** stands at no. 20 North (street addresses change from south to north when you cross Madison St.). Utility magnate Samuel Insull built it in the 1920s to house a 3,500-seat opera house and a 900-seat theater in an office building where rents would subsidize the arts. The Grand Foyer of the opera house, with its 40-foot-high ceiling, is worth a peek when the building is open; the opera season begins in late September.

Continue north and follow Wacker Drive as it bends to the east. At the midpoint of that bend is:

3. **333 W. Wacker Dr.** Always a crowd-pleaser, the facade of this building, by Kohn Pedersen Fox, suggests a massive, convex, green-tinted, multipaned looking glass—or a magnified fly's eye, highly stylized.

The building's curved exterior echoes the curve in the Chicago River, and the best views of the magic reflections cast by this glassy cladding are from the middle of the river. How do you stand in the middle of the river? On a boat, ideally an architectural river tour organized by the **Chicago Architecture Foundation** (☎ 312/922-3432). As the boat approaches 333 W. Wacker from either direction, a grand visual pageant unfolds upon the building's mirrored surface, where the cityscape and skyline to your rear are projected in an unbroken, filmlike continuum.

Lacking a boat to stand on, walk out on the Franklin Street Bridge, a stationary vantage point from which you can witness something of the same hypnotic effect.

The building's winning design is all the more remarkable when you consider that this 36-story tower had to be squeezed onto a rather awkward triangular plot that was previously thought suitable only for a parking lot.

Across the river is:

4. **The Merchandise Mart.** Touted as the world's largest commercial building, containing some 4.1 million square feet of rentable space, the Mart is a Chicago landmark as much for its place in the saga of American merchandising as for its hulking institutional presence. The building was completed in 1931; the few sparse elements of design that grace its asylumlike facade are discreetly deco. Marshall Field built the Mart as a wholesale emporium, and Joseph P. Kennedy (JFK's dad) bought it in 1945. The Kennedy family recently sold the building (Christopher Kennedy remains an executive vice president). Today it serves as a showcase for dealers of furniture and furnishings. Perched atop a line of pillars running the length of the building along the river pier are oversized busts of the icons of American merchandising, including Marshall Field, Edward A. Filene, George Huntington Hartford (A&P), Frank Winfield Woolworth, Julius Rosenwald (Sears), John N. Wanamaker, and Aaron Montgomery Ward (on a visit here, David Letterman aptly described them as giant PEZ dispensers).

Return across the Franklin Street Bridge to Wacker Drive, and keep walking east 2 blocks until you reach LaSalle Street. Turn right and continue south two blocks, passing under the El tracks, to Randolph Street. Now turn left (east) on Randolph Street and walk a half block; you will be standing before:

5. **The James R. Thompson Center.** This postmodern cascade of glass and steel is, depending on your point of view, the masterwork or folly of the celebrated contemporary architect Helmut Jahn. Within its million-plus-square-foot interior, the building shelters the Chicago branches of the state's many-tiered bureaucracy. On every floor, the transparent glass walls that enclose the offices allow citizens to observe their tax dollars at work. You'll hear Chicagoans call this building by its original name, the State of Illinois Building.

One theme said to underlie the architect's design is a symbolic reference to "open government," with its implied invitation for the public to come in and feel welcome. But the vast rotunda that greets you on entering doesn't require any subliminal manipulation to entice the public. The appeal of this vast beehivelike atrium, which rises the full 17 floors of the building, is self-evident. You're welcome to ride the glass elevator to the top of the building and take a look, but even borderline acrophobes may not want to linger at the dizzying perch. Near the main entrance, the Illinois Bureau of Tourism operates an information desk where you can ask for travel information and pick up brochures. On the plaza facing Randolph Street stands a public sculpture by Jean Dubuffet (see Walking Tour 2, "The Loop: Sculpture Tour").

Now cross Randolph Street and head south along Clark Street. The squat, many-columned, twin structure occupying the block encompassed by Clark, Randolph, LaSalle, and Washington streets is the:

6. **City Hall/County Building.** City Hall fronts LaSalle Street. The County Building, the older and more classical in appearance of the two government centers, faces Clark Street, where you should now be standing. Like many of the public edifices erected in the early years of the 20th century, the County Building is typically beaux arts in its classical appointments. It was designed in part by one of Chicago's legendary architectural firms, Holabird & Roche. Especially worthy of note are the Corinthian columns gracing the facade; at 75 feet, they're the largest columns constructed in the city of Chicago. The massive capitals topping each column are themselves the height of a single floor, and, as purely decorative additions, are supported by caissons 10 feet in diameter.

Across Clark Street, fronting a broad plaza along Washington Street, is:

7. **The Richard J. Daley Center.** This structure was named for the legendary mayor (and father of the current one) and longtime czar of Cook County politics. You can be excused for thinking that this tall, boxy monolith is the work of the late Ludwig Mies van der Rohe, dean of the Second Chicago School of Architecture. It is not. The building copies his idiom but is merely a "wannabe." The

singular characteristic of the Daley Center, completed in 1965, is that, despite its 648-foot height, the building has only 31 stories.

The number-one tourist photo opportunity in Chicago is to pose before the untitled Picasso sculpture, in residence on Daley Plaza since 1967.

Cross the plaza and walk east on Randolph Street, where you will enter the city's redeveloping:

8. **Theater District.** While many of the theaters that once lit up Randolph Street have been razed, a few remain. They form a row that has long been a dream of city planners: Looking back west, you'll see the marquee of the Cadillac Palace Theatre, and ahead of you, the fantastic sign of the Oriental Theatre. Both were former movie palaces; they reopened in the late 1990s after multimillion-dollar renovations that turned them into performing arts centers for touring musicals, dance performances, and concerts. With an over-the-top Indian-inspired theme, the Oriental (now known as the Ford Center for the Performing Arts) is a spectacular space well worth the price of admission for whatever is playing on stage. Ahead to your left, up State Street, you can't miss the nostalgic orange-lettered marquee of the Chicago Theatre. The magnificent theater was once the jewel in the crown of the Balaban & Katz movie theater empire. Designed by Rapp & Rapp, the 3,800-seat hall opened in 1928. The beaux arts theater was restored in 1986 as a showplace for Broadway musicals, concerts, and stage shows. The big question remains whether producers can find enough appealing shows to sell tickets to keep those big marquees burning bright. Joining them, on the corner of Randolph and Dearborn, are the dazzling new digs of the Goodman Theatre, the city's oldest resident theater. For decades, it occupied a facility attached to the Art Institute. In 2000, it moved to these state-of-the-art quarters, which includes 850- and 400-seat theaters, and an attached retail and restaurant mall where patrons can go for pre- and post-theater food and libations. The new Goodman is especially welcome because it returns a theater to this corner, once notably occupied by the Garrick Theater, designed

by Louis Sullivan, and because it incorporates the historic facades of the Harris and Selwyn theaters.

The redevelopment makes ever more gaping the open space on your right known as Block 37. An entire city block, it became something of an open wound in the city center when it was largely cleared in the 1980s for an office complex that went unbuilt. Some creative thinking has given the land a dual role—open-air ice rink in the winter, and tented home to a youth art program in the summer—until developers and the city settle on a plan for the block.

As you walk down State Street, you pass Chicago's version of Harrods, the block-long Marshall Field's flagship (stop in to glimpse the giant dome of Tiffany glass topping the central atrium). After a shopping interlude that could cost you a few hours, cross Washington Street. At 32 N. State St. is the historic entrance to the:

9. **Reliance Building.** A relic of the early days of the First Chicago School of Architecture, the Reliance Building is seen today as a prototype of the modern skyscraper. The simultaneous development of high-speed elevators and steel framing made its height possible. The building's foundation and base were constructed in 1891, the work of John Wellborn Root, who died that year before the building could be completed. Root's partner, Daniel Burnham, finally finished the Reliance Building in 1895 with the help of a new designer, Charles Atwood. Burnham is also remembered as the chief architect of the 1893 World's Columbian Exposition and as the creator of the 1909 Plan of Chicago (a sweeping blueprint, only partially implemented, for revamping the city's streets, parks, and plazas). Atwood is credited both with the decision to employ so much glass on the terra-cotta facade, which gives the building its modern appearance, and with the design of what would later be known as the Chicago Window—a large central pane of glass flanked by two smaller, double-hung windows used for ventilation. After a meticulous renovation, the building is now home to the Hotel Burnham, a 122-room boutique hotel. For a closer look at the renovation efforts, pass through the hotel

lobby to the building's splendid marble lobby; it's also possible to take an elevator up to look at the upper floors (those above the 8th floor are original).

The next stop showcases the work of Louis Henri Sullivan. Sullivan embodied the romantic spirit of Chicago architecture, and his lyrical vision was a counterpoint to the pure utilitarianism of his many contemporaries. He significantly influenced Frank Lloyd Wright, who apprenticed in his firm. Cross State Street and continue to the southeast corner of East Madison Street. There, at 1 S. State St., stands the magnificent facade of:

10. **Carson Pirie Scott & Co.** This building still houses one of Chicago's oldest department stores, which retains a hint of the elegance of bygone days. In designing a home for this vast emporium, Sullivan was required to consider the need for horizontal and open interior spaces. Two of his design features prevented the building from imitating the shoebox and warehouse style that typified the other State Street department stores of that period. Firstly, Sullivan placed the entrance at the corner of the building, below a multistoried tower that combines the visual and technical effects of a skyscraper. And finally, the poet in Sullivan would not allow the building to stand unadorned. The ornate metalwork, particularly above the entrance, suggests what one critic termed "a kind of poetic representation of nature capable of offsetting the materialist culture of an industrialized modern city."

Here is a good place to observe the makeover that has attempted to put some of the greatness back into State Street. Once a bustling avenue where generations of Chicagoans did their shopping in big-name department stores, it has suffered the slow loss of the big names and their customers to the suburbs. In the 1970s city officials attempted to reverse the decline by turning the street into a dedicated bus transitway. In the latest urban-planning tinkering, the street was "de-malled": The sidewalks were narrowed to create denser street life; new planters and reproduction vintage street lights were added to give the street a 1920s feel; and the street was reintegrated into the downtown grid, allowing cars to flow freely. You can judge for yourself, but many Chicagoans seem to agree that the changes have made the street a safer and more vibrant place to walk, shop, and go about their business.

Notice the **Chicago Building** on the corner, just across from Carson Pirie Scott at 7 W. Madison. The building dates from 1904, and makes full use of the Chicago Window motif on the facades of its exterior walls. Notice too how the original cornice runs unbroken along the top of the roofline, an unusual feature among Chicago buildings of this vintage, which were often subjected to renovation and alteration. Cross State Street and continue west down Madison Street. Turn left on Dearborn and continue south for 1 block. On the northeast corner at 30 W. Monroe St. is the:

11. **Inland Steel Building.** One of the first major buildings put up after a 20-year construction hiatus, Inland Steel was completed in 1958, and the building boasts many firsts for Chicago in its engineering and design. For example, all of its "mechanicals"—elevators and risers for plumbing, heating, and ventilation—are in the eastern tower. The building also shows off the advances in steel manufacturing that took place during World War II. Behind its shimmering, stainless steel cladding are invisible supports, steel pilings driven through 85 feet of swampy Loop soil into bedrock. Inland Steel was the first air-conditioned building in Chicago, the first to double-glaze its windows, and the first to offer indoor parking below street level. Finally, the soft glimmer of the floor-to-ceiling, emerald green windows creates an effect of post-modern eclecticism; the building seems contemporary because it was once so ahead of its time.

Across Dearborn Street, the sunken plaza around the giant Bank One Building is a favorite lunchtime gathering spot for those who work in the Loop. A fountain and another of Chicago's well-known public sculptures, *The Four Seasons* by Marc Chagall, also grace this outdoor sanctuary. Walking along the plaza side of Dearborn Street, continue south 1 block to Adams Street.

Take a Break An ideal spot for a midday pick-me-up or a light snack is the barroom at **The Berghoff** (☎ 312/427-3170), 1 block east (toward State St.) at 17

W. Adams St. The rathskeller-style tavern serves several Berghoff beers on tap, many other alcoholic and nonalcoholic beverages (including a tasty draft root beer), wursts, and sandwiches. The stand-up bar was the first in Chicago to get a liquor license after the end of Prohibition. For a moderately priced full meal from the lunch or dinner menu, you will have to take a seat in the restaurant itself, a Chicago landmark that celebrated its centennial in 1998. It's open Monday to Friday from 11am to 9pm, and Saturday from 11:30am to 10pm.

Now retrace your steps west along Adams Street and cross to the northwest corner of the intersection with Dearborn, where the tour continues at 140 S. Dearborn St., the:

12. **Marquette Building.** Considerable lore—historical and architectural—attends this early example of the commercial Chicago high-rise, which opened in 1895. Its name honors the Jesuit explorer Jacques Marquette, whose 1675 journal contains the first descriptions by a European of the site that would become Chicago. One of the building's original owners had translated Marquette's journal; he not only gave the priest's name to the edifice but also memorialized the expedition by Marquette and his companion Louis Jolliet. A series of relief sculptures of the explorers and Native Americans tops the building's main portal and the elevators; elaborate travel scenes in mosaic designed by the Tiffany Glass Company appear throughout the marble-trimmed lobby.

Architecturally, the Marquette Building has undergone several major transformations. It gained a sixth bay on the west side in 1905, and a 17th floor in 1950. Note the original ornamental grill on one of the elevators on the balcony level; the others were replaced to meet fire code years ago. Mies van der Rohe suggested a more abstract transformation when he was contemplating the design of the Chicago Federal Center, a complex of buildings across Adams Street flanking both sides of Dearborn. Rohe saw the Marquette as the "fourth wall" of his three-cornered complex. He used this theme as a point of departure for updating the Chicago commercial style, and the geographical point where the First and Second Chicago Schools of Architecture were to meet. In the spacious public plaza at the center of this constellation stands the vermilion stabile *Flamingo,* designed by Alexander Calder.

Follow Adams Street 2 blocks west to LaSalle Street. At this intersection, on diagonally opposite corners, are two of the most impressive buildings in Chicago. To fully appreciate them, you must enter them. First, on the northwest corner of LaSalle and Adams, is a building known simply as:

13. **190 S. LaSalle St.** This building is the only work in Chicago by Philip Johnson, an early acolyte of Walter Gropius, the Bauhaus grandmeister. Gropius was a refugee from Nazi Germany who traded his career in practical architecture for a teaching position at Harvard, where Johnson was his student. Nothing could be further from the rigid functionalism of the early Bauhaus school than the gothic splendor of this building's lobby. Its barrel-vaulted arch and gold-leaf ceiling rival the central naves of many great European cathedrals in grandeur and scale. At the north end of the enormous main lobby, otherwise completely empty except for an unobtrusive security desk at the south end, is a giant bronze (you're forgiven if you guessed wood, too) sculpture; entitled *Chicago Fugue,* the piece by British sculptor Anthony Caro suggests some kind of millwork machinery from the Middle Ages. Off the south end of the lobby, with access to Adams Street, is a small "chapel." On the wall opposite this entrance hangs an elegant wool-and-linen tapestry by Helena Hernmarck depicting the unrealized proposal for a grand civic center detailed in Daniel Burnham's Chicago Plan.

The exterior of Johnson's 44-story tower is equally impressive. John Wellborn Root's Masonic Temple, long since demolished, inspired the building's overall design. The arched windows and doors echo Root's Rookery, across the way (see Stop 15, below). And while the simple and repetitive detail work of 190 S. LaSalle St.'s exterior walls is attractive, the top of the building is pure fantasy in the form of a many-gabled cottage, giving the building an unexpected air of country lane domesticity.

Before we continue, look up at the massive limestone building directly across LaSalle Street from where you were just standing. At 135 N. LaSalle St. stands the old:

14. **Field Building.** Commissioned by Marshall Field and opened in 1934, this was the last building constructed in the Loop for 21 years, a period when the combination of the Great Depression and World War II forestalled all construction on this scale. The Field Building stands on the site formerly occupied by the Home Insurance Building (1885), the work of William Le Baron Jenny, which some students of architecture believe to have been the first skyscraper. Don't miss the building's gleaming Art Deco interior: Shining and streamlined from the mirrored walkways to the nickel-plated mailboxes, it's one of the finest examples in the city.

Now cross LaSalle Street, walking toward the old Field Building, and then cross Adams Street and walk to 209 S. LaSalle St., the legendary:

15. **Rookery.** Of the more than two dozen buildings constructed in the Loop by the firm of Burnham and Root in the final 2 decades of the 19th century, only the Rookery—built between 1885 and 1888—remains. The name memorializes a long-demolished city hall building that once stood on the site, the roost of many pigeons and politicians. There is no finer relic of Old Chicago in the city. To begin with, the Rookery's rough granite base and many turrets were almost certainly influenced by the heavy Romanesque style of H. H. Richardson, whose work—with the exception of Glessner House in the historic Prairie Avenue District—has disappeared from Chicago.

Furthermore, all the buildings of any dimension raised during this period benefited from numerous advances in engineering and materials spurred by a heightened concern for fireproofing and a need to concentrate growth in an area of the city where real estate was both limited and in high demand. The Rookery, in this sense, represents a transition in Chicago architecture, combining thick load-bearing masonry walls at its base with innovative iron framing on the upper stories. With the introduction of plate glass, the framing allowed for larger windows and therefore more light and better ventilation.

Many eye-catching details make the Rookery one of the standout attractions on this tour. The building's exterior is the product of many fantasies, incorporating diverse influences—not only Romanesque, but Venetian and Moorish as well. One small detail that is easily overlooked is the fancifully scripted street names embedded in stone on the corners of the building. But the real treat here—and this is why it is so important to visit the Rookery when the building is open—is the incredible inner court, a tour de force of design wrought in iron, copper, marble, glass, and terra-cotta, among other materials.

The Rookery is essentially a square built around an open interior court that rises the full height of the building's 11 stories. A lovely domed skylight covers the ground and mezzanine levels (for safety reasons, a 2nd skylight has been added at roof level to enclose the entire light shaft). The two-tiered interior court surrounds a gracefully curved cast-iron stairwell just beyond the small lobby and a grand central staircase on the opposite wall. A balcony at mezzanine level joins the stairways, and a railing of delicate grillwork encircles them. Frank Lloyd Wright replaced Root's Victorian-style ornamentation throughout the light court in 1905. Wright gave the space a more geometric look, replacing much of the original ironwork, installing large rectangular planters, and substituting a compound of gilded marble for Root's terra-cotta cladding. A 1991 renovation restored the Rookery's much-altered exterior and interior to their turn-of-the-century elegance. It stripped the marble sheathing from one side of a column in the light court, revealing the original terra cotta; the effect is to make Wright's marble covering look like sheet rock over richly textured horsehair plaster. Walk upstairs and follow the staircase to get a glimpse of the Rookery's interior courtyard (the gilded ornamentation is further evidence of the thoroughness of the building's rehabilitation) and the sublime stairway spiraling upward.

At Jackson Boulevard, 1½ blocks south, LaSalle Street appears to dead end (it actually jogs around to the east) before the imposing structure of the:

16. **Chicago Board of Trade.** Here at 141 W. Jackson Blvd. is the city's temple (or, more appropriately, throne, as the building's general configuration suggests) to high finance. It's the house that corn and wheat built as westward migration transformed the great trans-Mississippi prairie into the nation's granary. On a more prosaic level, the Board of Trade shelters that raucous free-for-all known as the commodities exchange, a kind of roller derby in pinstripes.

Opened in 1930, the 45-floor Board of Trade enjoyed the distinction of being the Loop's tallest building for 25 years, until the Prudential Building at 130 E. Randolph St. eclipsed it. The setbacks of the Board of Trade's upper stories are typical of the Art Deco styling of the era. Along the building's rear (southern) wall, the 24-story postmodern addition, the work of Helmut Jahn, offers a strange complement. The repetition of a pyramid-shaped roof, the principal feature common to both buildings, maintains symmetry between the older structure and the addition. In its day, the Board of Trade was considered so tall that the sleek aluminum sculpture adorning the building's peak, the Roman goddess of agriculture, Ceres, was left faceless. The reasoning was that no one in a neighboring building would ever get high enough to see the face anyway.

Now head 2 blocks east along Jackson Boulevard to the southwest corner of Dearborn and Jackson. At 53 W. Jackson Blvd. is the:

17. **Monadnock Building.** This mass of stonework forms two buildings that occupy this entire narrow block all the way to Van Buren Street. Only 2 years separate the construction of these architectural twins, but they are light years apart in design and engineering. You'll need to step across Dearborn to fully appreciate the differences.

Monadnock I, on the northern end, was built by Burnham and Root between 1889 and 1891. Note the deeply recessed windows at street level; walls of masonry 6 to 8 feet thick encase them. The building's facade curls gently down from the roof line in what architects call a "papyrus" design, an accommodation in the proportion of a structure of this elevation that required extra thickness at the base to support it.

Monadnock II, on the southern wing, was built by Holabird & Roche in 1893. Although the steel-framed building's design maintains continuity to some degree, somehow the effect is less satisfying than the original. It's especially pleasing to see that the building's current owner has selected signage and tenants (tobacco shop, bakery, and so forth) in keeping with the Monadnock's epoch.

Across the street, 1 block south at 343 S. Dearborn St., at the corner of Van Buren Street, is the:

18. **Fisher Building.** Daniel Burnham built this little gem in 1896 for developer Lucius Fisher. The patina of yellow terra-cotta sheathing is an attractive feature of the building's facade, as are the stern gothic adornments. Fisher ensured his own brand of immortality by having his architect include aquatic figures on the facade—delightful little fish, snakes, shells, and crabs. Details worth seeing on the third floor are the original floor mosaics and the walls of Carrara marble. The building's north side gained a bay in 1907; it seems to have buttressed the older section, which leans perceptibly in that direction owing to its less-than-firm foundation. The building's history was an obvious selling point when it was thoroughly renovated and converted into luxury apartments in 2000.

Continue down Dearborn Street, taking in a few more priceless samples of old Chicago architecture as this tour nears its final stop. Across Van Buren at 407 S. Dearborn St. is the:

19. **Old Colony Building.** Plymouth Street runs parallel to Dearborn here, 1 block east. In this street's name, and in the names of several vintage buildings throughout this old downtown section, we hear echoes of nostalgia for the New England origins of many pioneer Chicago families. The firm of Holabird & Roche completed the Old Colony in 1894. Among the building's standout features are the corner bays flanking the central tower, a variation on the tripartite design typical of many buildings of this era. The building's broad front gives a deceptive

impression of its bulk; when you turn the corner, you see it is only one bay wide. To achieve stability in the 17-story building, the architects included portal arches, a first in American construction.

At 431 S. Dearborn St., at the southeast corner of Congress Parkway, is the:

20. **Manhattan Building.** Constructed in 1891 by William Le Baron Jenny, this broad structure was viewed as an architectural wonder by many who visited Chicago during the Columbian Exposition 2 years later. To some, the eclectic use of materials and varied design of the facade give the Manhattan Building an appearance of complete chaos; others perceive a dynamic rhythm in the architect's choices. Whatever your aesthetic reaction, the Manhattan Building occupies a revered place in the annals of U.S. architecture: it was the first 16-story building in America, and for a time the tallest building in the world. In 1982, the Manhattan Building was renovated into apartments; it now includes condo units as well.

As many people do, you may be wondering about the curious triangular tower, carved with slivers of windows, that's visible a couple of blocks west, toward the Sears Tower. An interesting building to look at, yes, but you wouldn't want to visit. At West Van Buren and South Clark streets, it's the:

21. **Metropolitan Correctional Center.** Harry Weese designed this 27-story smooth concrete-clad building in 1975 as a jail for defendants preparing for trial in federal court. The building's three-sided form derives from an attempt by the U.S. Bureau of Prisons to reform prison conditions; cells surround a common lounge area from which unarmed guards monitor the inmates. The design apparently has been so successful that it's been copied in other facilities. There's not much chance of anybody breaking out: the windows are only 5 inches wide (and have bars, to boot), and wire mesh encloses the roof-deck recreational yard from above.

Continuing down South Dearborn Street, you cross Congress Parkway and enter the South Loop. This final stretch of Dearborn Street is a veritable museum of old Chicago architecture, featuring many fine early industrial buildings. This area is Printers Row, and was once the center of Chicago's printing industry. Over the last 2 decades, the neighborhood has become gentrified; along the route as you proceed south, you will pass a number of interesting shops and restaurants. At the end of the road is the:

22. **Dearborn Station.** This is Chicago's oldest surviving railroad station, a U-shaped Romanesque structure with a central clock tower. Today the station houses a variety of retail shops and food vendors, but there is nothing really special for a visitor.

    Retrace your steps up South Dearborn Street, turn right on West Van Buren Street, and you'll come to the final destination of the tour, the monumental:

23. **Harold Washington Library Center,** 400 S. State St. The construction of this imposing block-size building, the world's largest municipal library, concluded a disgraceful period in which the city's main library was shunted around town to various warehouses after it outgrew its original home in what's now the Chicago Cultural Center. Named for the city's first black mayor, the library was completed in 1991 by a firm led by Thomas Beeby, then dean of Yale University's School of Architecture. It's easy to mistake the library for a much older building, but the modern glass wall on the Plymouth Court side is a giveaway. With its thick walls and rusticated arches, the library pays homage to Chicago's First School of Architecture, echoing some of the forms of the Auditorium Building a few blocks east on Congress. The self-conscious mimicry disappointed some critics, who would have preferred a building that looked to the future and said something more about the city than playing up its past. On the other hand, fans seem comforted and delighted by the building's historicism and its whimsical ornamentation, which includes gargantuan owls perched on the roof, and cherubs puffing air in homage to the Windy City. Inside, the library has a handsome, though not grand, entryway that's not especially easy to navigate. Escalators connect to the building's 10 levels, where you'll find 1.8 million books and 14,000 periodicals, a large children's library, a 385-seat auditorium, and

plenty of computers with Internet connections. A generous portion of the building's $144 million price tag went to public art, and works by 55 artists, many of whom call the city home, adorn walls and passageways throughout.

Winding Down When you're ready to take a break, stop in the **Chicago Music Mart,** which runs along State Street between Van Buren and Jackson streets. The building is home to a number of music-themed shops, selling everything from pianos and sheet music to obscure CDs. You'll find a selection of casual eateries on the ground floor, including a deli and the **Blue Note Coffee Bar.** If you're lucky, you may find aspiring musicians giving an impromptu performance in the central lobby.

When you're done exploring, there are easy transportation options to speed you on your way, including the new Library/Van Buren El station flanking the library's north side and numerous buses on State Street.

The Loop: Sculpture Tour

Start: *Untitled,* by Pablo Picasso, in the Richard J. Daley Civic Center Plaza, on Washington Street between Dearborn and Clark streets.

Public Transportation: The Blue line stops at Washington and Dearborn, the Red line at Washington and State.

Finish: *The Fountain of the Great Lakes,* by Lorado Taft; Michigan Avenue near Jackson Drive.

Time: 2 to 3 hours.

Best Times: Virtually any time, within reason. Some sculptures are in building lobbies, which may be closed after business hours. At most times of year, early evening is not out of the question, because the streets are well traveled and well lit. While the Loop is safer and busier than ever after dark, it's still wise to be cautious and exercise common sense.

Among all major American cities, Chicago has led the way with its program of public art. Examples—traditional monuments, murals, and monumental contemporary sculpture—spread throughout the city, but their concentration within the Loop and nearby Grant Park has gradually transformed downtown Chicago into a "museum without walls."

Furthermore, while cities like Portland, Seattle, and Phoenix have initiated significant public art programs, no other municipality's collection even comes close to the scale and importance of Chicago's. In the Loop alone are representative works by many of the most celebrated artists and sculptors of the 20th century.

As in the field of architecture, Chicago public officials and city planners have demonstrated an unusual degree of foresight. They insist that growth in the public sphere—in the form of new construction and remodeling of municipal buildings—include some purely aesthetic contributions.

The city's Percent-for-Art ordinance calls for 1.33% of municipal building costs to be put aside for artwork, while the state and federal government also contribute. In recent years, many private companies have become voluntary partners in this program.

Our tour of this outdoor museum returns us to the Loop, but our focus will be entirely on the public art, rather than on the world-class architecture covered in Walking Tour 1, "The Loop: Chicago Architecture," and Walking Tour 3, "South Michigan Avenue & Grant Park." Some visitors may wish to combine these tours, or portions of them, into a single itinerary.

● ● ● ● ● ● ● ● ● ● ● ● ● ● ● ● ●

We begin in the Richard J. Daley Civic Center Plaza on Washington Street between Dearborn and Clark streets, before a sculpture whose image has become virtually synonymous with the city of Chicago:

1. ***Untitled*, by Pablo Picasso.** The artist donated this design to Chicago when he resolved not to cash the $100,000 check he received from the city. The 50-foot sculpture was executed in steel at a foundry on the city's south side from a maquette provided by Picasso, which is on display at the Art Institute. *Untitled* was installed at Daley Plaza in 1967 to a chorus of public disapproval. Outside a small circle of art sophisticates, the average philistine-in-the-street either hated the work outright or simply confessed to "not understanding" its obscure

The Loop: Sculpture Tour

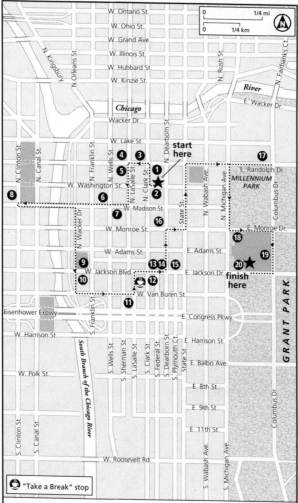

1 Untitled, by Pablo Picasso
2 Miró's Chicago
3 Monument with Standing Beast
4 Freeform
5 120 North LaSalle Street
6 Dawn Shadows
7 Loomings and Knights and Squires
8 Batcolumn
9 The Universe
10 Gem of the Lakes

11 San Marco II
12 The Town-Ho's Story
13 Ruins III
14 Flamingo
15 Lines in Four Directions
16 The Four Seasons
17 Untitled Sounding Sculpture
18 Large Interior Form
19 Celebration of the 200th Anniversary
of the Founding of the Republic
20 The Fountain of the Great Lakes

abstract "message." Clearly, the public had expected more from the great Picasso.

In time, the sculpture began to grow on people, like a homely mutt at the animal shelter whose sad eyes make an irrefutable case for instant adoption. As hearts and minds slowly warmed to *Untitled,* the notion began to circulate that the abstract work was indeed based on a model from reality—in fact, on two such images. Seen straight on, it was understood to be the likeness of Picasso's favorite hound, Kaboul; viewed from the side, it would seem to profile a woman.

With this concrete, if schizophrenic, identity intact, the sculpture, now affectionately embraced by citizens as "The Picasso," gradually assumed its semiofficial status as the logo of modern Chicago. It is one of the city's most popular photo opportunities for tourists.

The wide expanse of pavement known as Daley Plaza has become a favorite spot for public gatherings, lunchtime concerts, special events, flocks of pigeons, and skateboard enthusiasts, who execute "rail-slides" on the concrete curb at the base of the sculpture. When Chicagoans want to "tell it to City Hall," which is in the building across Clark Street, they organize demonstrations here. No public square would be complete without a war memorial: An eternal flame at one side of the plaza honors the veterans of Korea and Vietnam. Finally, the city sponsors a free cultural series (usually featuring music) at noon each weekday and, in season, a farmer's market twice a month on Thursdays. Because Picasso gave *Untitled* to the "people of Chicago," no one holds a copyright on the piece; as you can see, the sculpture is truly in the public domain.

Tucked into a confined plaza across the street next to the Brunswick Building (now housing Cook County offices), 69 W. Washington St., is:

2. **Miró's Chicago.** Like the Picasso, Joan Miró's design for this 39-foot statue of steel, wire mesh, concrete, bronze, and ceramic tiles was a gift to the city from the artist and was executed in Chicago. A cooperative effort involving the city and a group of private individuals raised $500,000 to produce it. Miró had a direct hand in the finished work, fabricating the ceramic tiles at his studio in

Majorca. They went into their designated spots soon after the concrete layering was sprayed onto the metal frame.

The statue is supposed to represent a great earth mother, but the reaction of one irate art student after the work's installation was less than maternal, or even fraternal: he splashed the rounded form with red paint. Most abstract art is an acquired taste, but this particular creation does look suspiciously like the Pillsbury Doughboy from the neck down. One very nice touch is the bronze plaque with the raised outline of the figure in Braille, allowing the blind to "see" the statue.

Note also the stained-glass windows in the building next door. This is the Chicago Temple, and at 568 feet it has the tallest church spire in the world, according to the *Guinness Book of World Records*. The First United Methodist Church maintains a sanctuary at street level and, in the spire above the intervening office space, a chapel. Free tours start weekdays at 2pm and Sunday at 9:30am and noon.

Now walk north 1 block along Clark Street to the James R. Thompson Center, 100 W. Randolph St., where you'll see a work by Jean Dubuffet:

3. ***Monument with Standing Beast ("Monument à la bête debout").*** This four-sided enclosure in fiberglass stands 29 feet at its highest point. Visitors may enter the structure. Completed in 1984, it represents what Dubuffet described as "drawing which extends . . . into space" to reach the man in the street. Dubuffet is best known for his "art brute," a creative interpretation of the brutality of the urban landscape, incorporating graffiti, street slang, and caricature. This work, donated to the city by private foundations, expresses four distinct motifs, none of which is especially harsh or hard-hitting. From one side you see an animal; from another a tree; a third view reveals a portal; and before the fourth wall, you face a gothic church.

The 16-story Thompson Center, designed by Helmut Jahn, rises above the Dubuffet. Specially commissioned artworks by Illinois artists are scattered throughout the expansive skylit rotunda. On the second floor of the building is the Illinois Art Gallery, featuring historical and contemporary works by state artists. The artisans' shop next door carries homegrown handicrafts. The glass-sided elevators, which run up the interior walls of the rotunda to the top floor, offer one of the city's great "rides."

Turn right as you exit the Thompson Center and walk around the building toward LaSalle Street. The Illinois State Office Building stands across the street at 160 N. LaSalle St. Adorning the facade is a work by Richard Hunt:

4. **Freeform.** The artist is a native son who has achieved international acclaim and trained at the School of the Art Institute. Completed in 1993, this sculpture is typical of his work, which embodies the idea of abstract art as something "freely formed" in the artist's pursuit of a unique mode of expression. The stainless-steel figure appears deceptively small but is 2½ stories high and weighs 3 tons. The building is an aging structure that was gutted and completely rejuvenated; the central bay, with its glassed-in courtlike lobby, is completely new.

You'll find two interesting examples of public art in Helmut Jahn's building half a block south, completed in 1991:

5. **120 N. LaSalle St.** The first is a fanciful mosaic by Roger Brown, *Art and Science of the Ancient World: The Flight of Daedalus and Icarus.* It arches above the entrance. Inside the lobby is a second work by Brown, a stylized cartoon portrayal of Chicago's equivalent of Wall Street, *LaSalle Corridor with Holding Pattern.* Another interesting piece inside the lobby is a cast bronze sculpture by Montana artist John Buck, *The Loop,* which brings life to Carl Sandburg's famous description of Chicago as the "City of the Big Shoulders."

Continue walking south 2 blocks and turn right, to the west, onto Madison Street. On the corner of Wells past the elevated tracks is a space called Madison Plaza. It holds a work by the incomparable Louise Nevelson:

6. **Dawn Shadows.** The superstructure of the elevated train reputedly inspired this expansive 30-foot-high composition in black painted steel, installed in 1983. The work is very different from the walls of stacked wooden

forms and boxes typically associated with Nevelson. Already near 80 when this public work was commissioned, she no doubt was also influenced considerably by the work of her contemporary Alexander Calder, and by a younger New York artist whose massive steel structures achieved explosive worldwide recognition in the 1970s, Richard Serra. Normally, Nevelson's work demonstrated more originality, a quality that carried over to her dramatic persona.

On the southeast corner of the intersection (diagonally across from *Dawn Shadows*) is the PaineWebber Tower, 181 W. Madison St. Adorning the lobby are two companion art pieces by sculptor Frank Stella:

7. **Loomings** and **Knights and Squires.** The construction firm of Miglin and Beitler, also responsible for the Nevelson sculpture across the street, commissioned these. J. Paul Beitler and the late Lee Miglin have prided themselves on their commitment to public art, and sculptures commissioned from well-known 20th-century artists adorn each of their buildings throughout Chicago. In planning this building, the developers specifically asked architect Cesar Pelli to design the five-story, 100-foot-long marble lobby as a gallery to display Stella's two works.

Frank Stella, whose international reputation began to soar in the late 1960s, describes the two pieces as "paintings." In fact, they are low-relief sculptures fabricated from aluminum and magnesium, then etched and brightly painted by the artist. The titles of these pieces place the sculptures in Stella's *Moby-Dick* series, begun in 1985 when the artist first sought inspiration in Herman Melville's epic tale. The three-dimensionality of the stunning sculptures invites close inspection from many angles.

The next work on our route is not within the Loop, but it's so large that you can catch a glimpse of it as you walk west along Madison Street. To see it up close, you must walk a fair distance west to Clinton Street, on the fringe of an area called Greek Town. True art aficionados may wish to hop a cab from downtown and have the driver cruise by Claes Oldenburg's unique and amusing:

8. **Batcolumn.** Oldenburg, a native of Sweden who grew up in Chicago, was one of the few practitioners of 1960s "Pop Art" who never seemed to take himself too seriously. And yet, the scale of conception of Oldenburg's works, which seem to poke fun at the very essence of American popular culture, elevates his vision to the realm of high art. The *Batcolumn,* in front of the Social Security Administration Building at 600 W. Madison St., is a prime example of Oldenburg's offbeat whimsy. Although the title of this piece suggests Batman, Oldenburg's foil is the revered national pastime, baseball. A 100-foot-high Louisville Slugger of latticed steel, propped up on a stubby cylindrical base, confronts the bewildered viewer.

Whether or not you treat yourself to this digression, our tour continues 2 blocks west on Madison and south along Wacker, where we enter the atrium lobby of the Sears Tower, 233 S. Wacker Dr., to see:

9. **The Universe.** This is a delightful moving wall sculpture—giant twirling flowers, swinging pendulum, and spinning sun—by Alexander Calder, installed here in 1974. For more about Calder, see Stop 14.

While we're in the neighborhood, we'll drop into the Wintergarden, the spectacular entryway to the building next door, 311 S. Wacker Dr. It contains a work by architect-turned-sculptor Raymond Kaskey:

10. **Gem of the Lakes.** The setting of this traditional sculpture commands the lion's share of one's appreciation. The bronze fountain with classical overtones dates to 1990 and occupies the vast, glass-roofed conservatory attached to the attractive, 65-story postmodern skyscraper. The Wintergarden occupies 12,000 square feet under an arched, multipaned glass roof 85 feet high. Two lines of giant palm trees border the pool, which is filled by water flowing from the fountain sculpture; on either side of the palms, two rows of stately columns support the roof and the walls of glass behind them.

Follow Van Buren Street east to the One Financial Place Plaza at 440 S. LaSalle St. At the back of the plaza, you'll see a bronze horse created by Ludovico de Luigi:

11. **San Marco II.** The model for Luigi's bronze was a set of four horses that once graced the facade of St. Mark's Basilica in Venice (the originals eventually decayed, and reproductions replaced them). Sculpted in Constantinople, the statues came to Venice around 1200, spoils from the Fourth Crusade. As an homage to this "destroyed treasure of his native city," Ludovico de Luigi executed *San Marco II.* The horse, posed in midstride, stands atop a fountain outside the current headquarters of the Chicago Stock Exchange.

> **☕ Winding Down** For a late afternoon cocktail, try the clubby **Jesse Livermore's,** 401 S. LaSalle St. In this lounge across the street from the Board of Trade, you'll find wheeler-dealers unwinding, surrounded by dark-paneled walls, a fireplace, and classical music.

Walk 1 block north and east to 77 W. Jackson Blvd., the Ralph H. Metcalfe Federal Building. The lobby contains another example of Frank Stella's work, a monumental sculpture called:

12. **The Town-Ho's Story.** Also part of Stella's *Moby-Dick* series, this 18-foot colossus on a 14-foot-wide base is a "collage" of several smaller statues, which the artist welded into one large abstract shape. That became a frame over which Stella poured molten aluminum to achieve this final "enhanced" shape. According to Melville scholar Robert K. Wallace, the sculpture takes its name "from a chapter of Melville's novel that is a tale about Steelkilt, an audacious sailor who uses both mind and fist to resist mistreatment." Dating from 1993, the work was commissioned by the federal General Services Administration through its Art-in-Architecture program. The sheer volume of space in the lobby of the Metcalfe Building dictated, in part, the scale Stella chose for his final design.

Directly across the street, outdoors on the northeast corner of Jackson Boulevard and Clark Street, is a sculpture called:

13. **Ruins III.** This concrete and bronze ensemble of forms, the work of sculptor Nita K. Sunderland, was installed in

1978. While considerably less ambitious than the grander displays of public art within the Loop, in many ways this piece is as appealing as any of them. It presents a nice counterpoint to the massive scale of the surrounding office towers.

Farther east on Jackson Boulevard, you will come to Federal Center Plaza, which fronts Dearborn Street. Here, stretched across the pavement, stands Alexander Calder's vermilion-colored masterpiece:

14. **Flamingo.** You might imagine that this construction would have been more aptly named *Praying Mantis*. But, as Calder observed, his stabiles have no reference to actual forms. He chose the name because the piece "was sort of pink and has a long neck." With this single fluid mass of steel rising 53 feet into the air, the artist somehow managed to transform an otherwise sterile plaza into a space more hospitable to the human species. Great numbers traffic this plaza daily, but the workday rush slackens to the pace of a Sunday stroll through an English park when people pass beneath the spreading limbs of Calder's stabile. Look for his initials inscribed on one of the northern legs.

As you walk east on Jackson, set back from the street in a small inlet (approximately across from 19 W. Jackson Blvd.) is the work of another minimalist artist, Sol Lewitt, whose success has allowed him to express his ideas on a monumental scale:

15. **Lines in Four Directions.** The work is a 90-by-72-foot relief sculpture nearly eight stories high, installed in 1985 on the brick wall of a small building facing the east facade of the Dirksen Federal Building. It's a screen of white-painted aluminum slats arranged in geometric patterns and projecting 2 inches from the wall, divided into four equal sections. This "wall project" is a realization in three dimensions of a drawing from a series Lewitt has been working with since 1968.

Return to Dearborn Street and walk 2 blocks north to the northwest corner at Monroe, where in the midst of a recessed space called Bank One Plaza is a work by Marc Chagall:

16. **The Four Seasons.** The piece is a rectangular mono-
    lith of concrete, sheathed with a mosaic of pastel-
    colored stone and glass fragments. The six fanciful scenes
    of Chicago seem to float on the surface of the huge
    box, 70 feet long, 10 feet wide, and 14 feet high, in the
    perspectiveless manner so characteristic of Chagall. The
    sculpture was executed in Chicago, but Chagall had
    worked out the designs at his studio in France, transfer-
    ring his vision onto full-sized panels, using a palate of 250
    colors. This space around the Bank One Building is one
    of the most popular public plazas in downtown Chicago,
    especially at lunchtime and after work during warm
    weather.

    Continue east on Monroe until you reach State Street;
    from here walk north to Madison. Take in the orna-
    mental facade of the Carson Pirie Scott & Co. depart-
    ment store, the work of Louis Sullivan, on the southeast
    corner of State and Madison streets. This work is dis-
    cussed more fully in Walking Tour 1, "The Loop: Chicago
    Architecture," but it never suffers from overexposure.

    Now proceed north 2 blocks, then go east for 2 blocks
    along Randolph Street. Cross Michigan Avenue and walk
    to 200 E. Randolph St. On the east and west sides of the
    Aon Building Plaza, adjoining the second tallest building
    in Chicago, is a pair of identical environmental sculptures
    designed by Harry Bertoia:

17. **Untitled Sounding Sculpture.** The units of thin
    copper rods stand upright in a reflecting pool. The wind
    activates them and they vibrate at different frequencies,
    producing pleasing musical tones. Bertoia's image for this
    work recalls fields of wheat blowing in the wind, com-
    bined with the mythological notion of the Aeolian harp.
    The artist came to the United States from Italy at the age
    of 15 and later studied architecture under the Finnish
    master Eliel Saarinen. Harry Bertoia is best known for the
    celebrated wire chair he designed in 1952. This site is also
    a good vantage point from which to gaze back upon the
    Michigan Avenue skyline.

    Return to Michigan Avenue and walk south. On this
    stretch of parkland the city provides space each year for

temporary sculptural exhibitions, including the weighty human bronzes of Fernando Botero and a giant 100-foot-long picnic table called *Running Table* by Dan Peterman.

Across Monroe Street, in a space at the foot of the Art Institute called the Stanley McCormick Memorial Court, is a tall bronze sculpture designed by Henry Moore:

18. **Large Interior Form.** This work, installed in 1983, is a separate cast of the "inner element" of a larger construction in the lobby of Three First National Plaza, called *Large Upright Internal/External Form.* Both works explore the sensuality inherent in natural forms, an infatuation at the core of Moore's lifelong curiosity to understand "what three-dimensionality is all about."

Moore, the son of a Yorkshire coal miner, won a scholarship to study at London's Royal College of Art. He suggests that much of the inspiration for his work came from the collections of primitive non-Western sculpture in the British Museum, which the young art student often visited in his spare time. Moore preferred to create sculptures for the outdoors. There are four additional examples of his work, in natural settings, throughout Chicago and its environs: *Nuclear Energy* and *Reclining Figure* at the University of Chicago, *Sundial* at the Adler Planetarium, and *Large Two Forms* at the Gould Center in Rolling Meadows.

Another world-class name in sculpture, Isamu Noguchi, is represented in Chicago with his work in Grant Park, on the east facade of the Art Institute complex at Columbus Drive between Monroe Street and Jackson Drive. The work goes by the long name of:

19. **Celebration of the 200th Anniversary of the Founding of the Republic.** The California-born Noguchi's work was installed in 1976 to commemorate the American Bicentennial. The highly stylized fountain "integrates the visual poetry of a Japanese garden with the precision of modern technology." The entire work is shaped from 3-million-year-old rainbow granite quarried in Minnesota. Other than the pool, the two principal elements of this construction are an upright, L-shaped pillar and a low horizontal cylinder, split down the

middle; both are vehicles for water, which flows into the surrounding basin. The first form represents a tree, the second a natural spring.

No tour of Chicago's public art would be complete without acknowledging Illinois native Lorado Taft, whose works adorn many quarters of the city. This tour will end in the rear of the courtyard on Michigan Avenue near Jackson Drive, with this example of Taft's exceptional talent:

20. **The Fountain of the Great Lakes.** Taft credits the inspiration for this work to a remark by architect Daniel H. Burnham, who said that no one had ever personified the Great Lakes in a work of art. When Taft received a commission by the Art Institute to create a public fountain, he also accepted Burnham's challenge and chose a classical theme to carry it out. The mythological story of the Danaides, 49 beautiful sisters who were doomed for eternity to carry water in sieves, suggested to Taft the idea of five classical female figures carrying conch shells, and positioned in such a way that water flows from one shell to another. In the sculptor's words, "'Superior' on high and 'Michigan' on the side both empty into the basin of 'Huron' who sends the stream to 'Erie' whence 'Ontario' receives it. . . ." Taft, who grew up in Elmwood, Illinois, first made his mark internationally at the 1893 World's Columbian Exposition.

South Michigan Avenue & Grant Park

Start: Chicago Cultural Center, 78 E. Washington St., at South Michigan Avenue.

Public Transportation: Take the Brown, Green, Purple, or Orange line to the Madison/Wabash stop, or the Red line to the Washington/State stop. Buses passing along South Michigan Avenue or nearby include nos. 3, 4, 60, 145, 147, or 151.

Finish: The Art Institute of Chicago, South Michigan Avenue at Adams Street.

Time: 2 to 4 hours.

Best Times: A warm, open-ended summer day or a weekend practically any time of year, weather permitting. If your walk will include visits to museums or attractions, plan around their open hours.

Worst Times: Only nighttime is unsuitable for this itinerary. No sensible person enters an urban park after dark (unless accompanied by a large multitude going to an event).

T his walk follows Michigan Avenue south to Balbo Avenue. It's as close as you can get in Chicago to a stroll along a grand boulevard, with pauses for you to take in various sites of cultural, historical, and architectural interest. If you choose, you can then walk (or take a cab) about a mile south to visit the Field Museum, Shedd Aquarium, and Adler Planetarium. The return to our point of departure takes you through Grant Park, the long patch of green space bordering Lake Michigan on one side and the Loop on the other. In its entirety, this walk not only provides a unique perspective on downtown Chicago, but it also takes visitors past the single largest concentration of cultural institutions in the city. You may decide to briefly "preview" some of these attractions now, or return later as interest and scheduling permit.

● ● ● ● ● ● ● ● ● ● ● ● ● ● ●

Begin at the:

1. **Chicago Cultural Center,** promoted as the "People's Palace." There are many reasons to visit what was formerly the main branch of the Chicago Public Library.

   Enter the building, which dates from 1897, from Washington Street, and take in the workmanship of the breathtaking lobby. Most of the first floor on this side of the building houses the Museum of Broadcast Communications, which includes the Radio Hall of Fame and the Kraft Telecenter. Admission to the museum is free.

   The grand central staircase in the lobby leads to the Preston Bradley Hall on the third floor, another exquisite space used frequently for free public concerts and other performances. One floor below, down a modern passageway leading to the north half of the building, is a theater used primarily for films and live performances and as a meeting hall. Adjacent to the theater is the G.A.R. (Grand Army of the Republic) Rotunda. The glorious, ornate leaded dome, formerly a skylight, is artificially backlit to allow for full appreciation of its beauty and craftsmanship. There are also several galleries and exhibition spaces that feature an ever-changing lineup of art.

The ground floor on the Randolph Drive side of the Cultural Center contains a large cafe, a Visitor Information Center operated by the Chicago Office of Tourism, a gift shop, a dance studio used for classes and free public performances, and a gallery with a permanent exhibit of architectural photography known as Landmark Chicago. Free docent-led tours of the building begin at 1:15pm Wednesday, Friday, and Saturday. The Chicago Cultural Center's hours are Monday to Wednesday from 10am to 7pm, Thursday 10am to 9pm, Friday 10am to 6pm, Saturday 10am to 5pm, and Sunday 11am to 5pm; closed holidays.

Starting Out **The Corner Bakery** at the Chicago Cultural Center is the perfect spot to hang out over a cup of gourmet coffee and a light snack while you get your bearings before plunging into this walking tour. If you're visiting on a weekday, plan your visit around the lunch hour to take in a free concert, from classical to country, at 12:15pm. In warm weather, there's outdoor seating along Randolph Street.

When you exit the building and turn onto Michigan Avenue, your eyes will no doubt be drawn across the street to one of the most eagerly awaited, most expensive, most ambitious new attractions in the city:

2. **Millennium Park.** Our current mayor, Richard Daley, had grand plans for this dramatic new extension of Grant Park, which was due to open in 2000. Three years and hundreds of millions of dollars later, it is finally taking shape. Between formal gardens and promenades are scattered an underground theater for music and dance troupes, a skating rink along Michigan Avenue, and an enormous polished stainless steel, elliptical sculpture that was the first U.S. commission for Indian-born sculptor Anish Kapoor. Most notably, the park will contain a dramatic new music pavilion designed by superstar architect Frank Gehry. Designs show a flashy ribbon-topped bandshell that will be the new home for the Grant Park Symphony Orchestra and other special events, and a building that many believe will instantly become one of the city's signature structures.

South Michigan Avenue & Grant Park

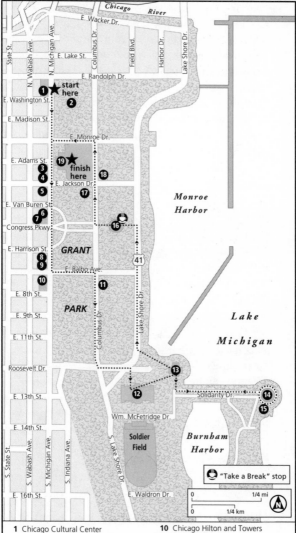

1 Chicago Cultural Center
2 Millennium Park
3 Theodore Thomas Orchestra Hall
4 Chicago Architecture Foundation
   Shop and Tour Center
5 Britannica Centre
6 Fine Arts Building
7 Auditorium Building
8 Spertus Museum
9 Blackstone Hotel

10 Chicago Hilton and Towers
11 Grant Park
12 Field Museum of Natural History
13 John G. Shedd Aquarium
14 Adler Planetarium
15 America's Courtyard
16 Clarence Buckingham Fountain
17 The Seated Lincoln
18 Petrillo Music Shell
19 The Art Institute of Chicago

Walk south 3 blocks on Michigan Avenue toward Adams Street. Along the way, you will pass several small buildings that might spark your curiosity. For example, Louis Sullivan designed the terra-cotta facade of the **Gage Building,** 18 S. Michigan Ave., at the behest of the Gage Brothers, who hoped that this burst of external beautification would "benefit" their millinery business. The gabled roof above the **Monroe Building,** 104 S. Michigan Ave., provides an eye-catching feature along the skyline. Take a peek inside to see the vaulted lobby. At 220 S. Michigan Ave. is the home of the Chicago Symphony Orchestra:

3. **Theodore Thomas Orchestra Hall.** Believing that the Chicago Symphony needed a home of its own, rather than continuing to share space at the Auditorium Building down the block, Daniel Burnham designed this building, which opened its doors in 1905. The facade is Georgian; inside, in addition to the orchestra hall, is a ballroom on the second floor, along with innumerable offices. With its official name, Orchestra Hall honors conductor and onetime violin prodigy Theodore Thomas, who is credited with founding symphony orchestras in many American cities—including Chicago's, in 1898. Thomas conducted the first U.S. performances of works by such contemporaries as Tchaikovsky, Brahms, and Johann Strauss. The 1997 to 1998 season inaugurated the $105 million Symphony Center, the new name for the musical complex that incorporates an acoustically and aesthetically enhanced Orchestra Hall, a new education wing, a 300-seat concert hall, and a fine-dining restaurant.

Next door at 224 S. Michigan Ave. is the:

4. **Chicago Architecture Center.** This is a don't-miss stop for an overview of the city's architecture and its significance. Run by the highly respected Chicago Architecture Foundation, the center is the starting point for many guided tours conducted by a corps of highly informative volunteer docents. The CitySpace gallery has exhibits on the city's architectural history (including video interviews with some of the world's most respected architects), and the shop is a great place to pick up classy Chicago souvenirs.

The center occupies a structure of some interest: the Santa Fe Center, known originally as the Railway Exchange Building, designed by the firm of D. H. Burnham & Co. As in the Rookery, a principal design feature here is a two-story skylit atrium whose walls are clad with decorative tiles molded from terra-cotta.

Across Jackson Boulevard at 310 S. Michigan Ave. is the:

5. **Britannica Centre.** The former Straus Building, sheathed in Indiana limestone, dates from 1924 and is home to the Encyclopaedia Britannica Company. The setback windows conform to conditions required by a 1923 zoning ordinance that allowed buildings in Chicago to rise above 260 feet for the first time. At night, the great glass beehive on the rooftop, symbol of the original banking firm, casts a blue light; four bison representing thrift, industry, strength, and city surround the hive. The Savvy Traveller, an outstanding specialty bookstore, occupies the ground floor.

Continue south for 1½ blocks, crossing Van Buren Street and stopping before 410 S. Michigan Ave., the:

6. **Fine Arts Building.** Perhaps no other building in Chicago has a more interesting and varied background. Originally called the Studebaker Building, it served as a five-floor showroom for that company's well-crafted carriages. Solon S. Berman, who laid out George Pullman's company town on the extreme southern edge of Chicago, constructed the building in 1885. In 1898, when the Studebaker Company vacated the building, it became an arts center, with two theaters on the ground floor, plus workspaces for a spectrum of artists and writers, including skylit studios in a new three-story addition. Among the Fine Arts Building's illustrious tenants over the years were Frank Lloyd Wright, the sculptor Lorado Taft, and, according to some sources, L. Frank Baum, author of *The Wonderful Wizard of Oz.*

Today, the building still houses many creative tenants. Inside you'll find some visual treats, like the marble-and wood-trimmed lobby, and a series of wall murals on the 10th floor (reached by old-fashioned human-operated elevators).

Next door to the Fine Arts Building is our next point of curiosity, 430 S. Michigan Ave., or the:

7. **Auditorium Building.** The team of Dankmar Adler and Louis Sullivan was responsible for this landmark of *fin de siècle* Chicago architecture. In a sense, theirs was a perfect partnership: Adler was a man of nuts-and-bolts business acumen, and Sullivan was a visionary of design. The staying power of their achievement and the Auditorium Building's elevated reputation rest on several factors. When it opened in 1889, the Auditorium was one of Chicago's first multiuse buildings; it contained a fine hotel, a theater, and, in a 17-story tower perched above the southwest corner of the roof, some of the most expensive office space in the city.

In its sheer mass and patently Richardsonian monumental scale, the Auditorium Building's general appearance is palpable testimony to the influence H. H. Richardson had over many architectural disciples, including Sullivan and John Wellborn Root. The building, which rises above a rusticated granite base, spreads between Michigan Avenue and Wabash. Sullivan's refined exterior work—the arched windows and other details of form that grace the Auditorium's facade—owes its greatest debt to the solid structural innovations introduced by his partner. Adler had perfected his craft while serving in the Union Army as an engineer during the Civil War.

The inauguration of the theater transformed the rough-cut city, still struggling to resurrect itself from the fire that had nearly destroyed it some 2 decades before, into a viable cultural center with international credentials. Some of Adler's original contributions involved engineering features in the theater itself. He encased the 4,300-seat theater in a shell of firebrick and configured the interior space with sight lines and acoustics that are still the envy of many modern entertainment halls. A wide stage with elaborate hydraulic equipment enhanced the epic quality of many performances, which had to be spectacular indeed to rival the beauty of Sullivan's decor. The Auditorium Theatre is still an important cultural venue, and tours of its interior take place regularly. For information on scheduling a tour, call ☎ **312/431-2354.**

Since 1949, Roosevelt University has occupied the Auditorium Building, so you're guaranteed access to some of the grand features of the former hotel during hours when classes are in session. The university library, for example, occupies the barrel-vaulted salon on the 10th floor that was the hotel's dining room, and is yet another showcase of the handiwork of Sullivan's gifted artisans. The library and the second-floor student lounge both offer stunning views of Buckingham Fountain, Grant Park, and the lake. Photographs on the north side of the lobby document some of the building's history.

Our tour continues south for another 2 blocks before entering Grant Park, so you can now cross Congress Parkway. Looking back, you may be able to notice where the southern bay of the original Auditorium Building, once the site of the hotel's long and elegant barroom, was demolished to make room for the expanded roadway. Another block down, across Harrison Street in one wing of Columbia College at 600 S. Michigan Ave., is the **Museum of Contemporary Photography.** It's open Monday to Friday from 10am to 5pm, Thursday until 8pm, and Saturday noon to 5pm; admission is free. Nearby at 618 S. Michigan Ave. is the:

8. **Spertus Museum.** Housed in the same building as the Spertus Institute of Jewish Studies, the museum's collection of some 10,000 works offers the public a sweeping view of Jewish culture as it has evolved over more than 3 millennia. Items on display include ceremonial objects, textiles and costumes, jewelry, coins, paintings, sculpture, and graphics from around the world. Many Chicago-area schools use workshops, films, and other resources at the Spertus Museum's Zell Holocaust Memorial to comply with a 1990 state law mandating Holocaust education in all Illinois public schools. Other programs at the museum include weekend film and lecture series. Hours are Sunday to Wednesday from 10am to 5pm, Thursday 10am to 7pm, Friday 10am to 3pm; closed Saturday. There is an admission fee every day except Friday.

The next cross street to the south is Balbo Avenue, where we will enter Grant Park. But first, take in the graceful structure on the corner at 636 S. Michigan Ave., the:

9. **Blackstone Hotel.** One of Chicago's original luxury hotels (built 1908–10), the Blackstone has figured in the worlds of literature and film. James T. Farrell used the hotel as a setting for a New Year's Eve party in *Studs Lonigan,* a trilogy about the lives of the Chicago Irish during the early years of the 20th century. More recently, the savage banquet scene in the movie *The Untouchables* was shot here. The Blackstone evoked the style of a similar hotel a few miles south, the Metropole, where Al Capone once resided and where such an event might have actually taken place. While the Blackstone languished in the 1990s, it was recently converted into ultra-expensive condos, returning this grande dame to its original splendor.

Now cross Balbo and check out the old Conrad Hilton, at 720 S. Michigan Ave. The first name in hotel swank throughout much of the 20th century, it's known today as the:

10. **Hilton Chicago.** The Hilton is a relic from the final days of the age of grandeur, when "putting on the Ritz" was considered the best revenge in a world of crumbling economic fortunes. Built as the 3,000-room Stevens Hotel in 1927, it was then the largest hotel in the world. Among its extravagant amenities, the Stevens offered its guests a 1,200-seat theater equipped for moving-picture "talkies," a private in-house hospital, an indoor ice rink, and a rooftop that included two gardens and the 18-hole High Ho Golf Course.

Today, these services have gone the way of all such excesses. But the modern Hilton is definitely worth a few moments; wander into the lobby and walk around a public space of rare elegance and dimension (sneak a peek into the Grand Ballroom if you can). Selections from the hotel's archives, displayed in the lobby area, are also worth a look; the hotel has hosted U.S. presidents, international royalty and an eclectic selection of 20th-century celebrities.

Cross South Michigan Avenue at the corner of Balbo. Our walking tour will now double back on itself via:

11. **Grant Park.** In July 1968, Norman Mailer, in town to cover the Democratic Presidential Convention, looked out the window of his room in the Hilton and reflected on the presence of thousands of Vietnam War protesters who were at that moment encamped in Grant Park, otherwise known as "Chicago's formal front garden." That brief episode sums up Grant Park's essential function: It is not so much a green space that imitates the idyllic environment of a woods or forest, but a checkerboard of great lawns, crisscrossed by broad roadways and train tracks, that serves as a giant outdoor arena for mass public events. Over a 10-week period in the summer, for example, popular outdoor concerts take place in the park Wednesday to Sunday evenings. These and other seasonal public festivals justify so many empty acres, which otherwise are not terribly parklike.

For our purposes, however, the park—especially on a quiet, nonfestival day—provides a contrast to the sidewalk strolling that has occupied the first half of this tour. From its middle ground, you'll get a unique perspective on the city, as if you were viewing the skyline of the Loop from a distant shore.

Enter the park along East Balbo Drive and walk the long block to the first wide thoroughfare, Columbus Drive. Here you have the option of walking the better part of a mile (the foot-weary should consider a taxi) to the southern extreme of the park to see or visit three of Chicago's most popular cultural institutions. You can also return north through the park to our tour's starting point; jump to Stop 14 if you choose to skip the southern end of Grant Park. This part of the walk has been improved considerably with the marvelous creation of a "Museum Campus," unifying the three institutions in a parkscape developed with the relocation of the northbound lanes of Lake Shore Drive.

Should you choose to walk south, the first building among the triad of cultural attractions is the:

12. **Field Museum of Natural History.** Combining a somewhat old-fashioned view of nature as a giant curio

shop with a contemporary emphasis on interactive show-manship, the Field is one of Chicago's most fascinating museums. Even on a walking tour, one can justify paying the price of admission and making a cursory inspection of the exhibits, enjoying whatever the eye can absorb during a brief visit. If you choose to remain outside, at least pause before the monumental temple to appreciate the harmony of its classical design. Daniel Burnham began the work around 1909, and derived his inspiration, as the telling line of Ionic columns confirms, from the Erechtheum (ca. 400 B.C.), one of the great shrines adorning the Acropolis in Athens. The museum is open daily from 9am to 5pm; admission is $8 for adults, $4 for children 3 to 11.

Directly east of the Field Museum, a short walk away, is an enterprise that is rapidly becoming the most popular tourist attraction in Chicago, the:

13. **John G. Shedd Aquarium.** There's a fantasy quality to the building that houses the aquarium, with its dozens of decorative aquatic figures. The meteoric rise in the attraction's popularity dates to the 1991 addition of the Oceanarium, a marine mammal pavilion re-creates a Pacific Northwest coastal environment, with a curtain wall at one end that incorporates Lake Michigan into its watery motif. Open daily from 9am to 6pm (until 5pm on winter weekdays); admission is $8 for adults, $6 for children (there's an extra charge for the Oceanarium).

Connected to the Shedd Aquarium in spirit if not theme is the:

14. **Adler Planetarium and Astronomy Museum,** on the east end of Solidarity Drive, a manmade causeway extending to a landfill known as Northerly Island. The zodiacal, 12-sided dome sits on a promontory facing the runway of its cotenant on this artificial landmass, Miegs Field, an airfield for small planes. Through a variety of programs, the planetarium brings the night sky into sharper focus for the human eye. The planetarium is open daily from 9:40am to 4:30pm; admission (including one show) is $13 for adults, $11 for children 4 to 17. The **Sky Show** is offered daily; call ☎ 312/922-STAR for times.

On the south lawn of the Adler is Chicago's answer to Stonehenge:

15. **America's Courtyard.** This circle of concentric stones, installed by Brazilian sculptors Denise Milan and Ary Perez, lines up for observation of the solstices and equinoxes that mark the change of seasons (a matter of much significance in a place like Chicago where the sun's whereabouts figures so prominently). No matter the season, the assemblage is a nice spot for relaxation and contemplation with the lake on one side, the skyline on the other. From here you can get a glimpse of private planes taking off and landing at Meigs Field, a small airport used by corporate executives and politicians who want a quick trip to downtown.

Now return to the vicinity of East Balbo Drive along one of three possible routes: on Columbus Drive, through the park, or along Lake Shore Drive, the route closest to Lake Michigan. Just north of Balbo Drive, you will see the approach to the:

16. **Clarence Buckingham Fountain.** This baroque fountain, constructed in pink Georgia marble, is the centerpiece of Grant Park. It's twice as large as its model, the Latona Fountain on the grounds of Versailles. Throughout the late spring and summer, the fountain spurts columns of water up to 165 feet in the air, illuminated after dark by a whirl of colored lights.

Take a Break   The addition of a pair of outdoor restaurants at Buckingham Fountain makes it an appealing place to while away a stretch of the afternoon. Both are open when the fountain operates (May 1–Oct 1, or later if the weather permits) from 10am to 11pm daily. **Buckingham Cafe and Grill** (☎ 312/922-6847) serves a menu of grilled panini (sandwiches), subs, burgers, dogs, desserts, coffee, and cappuccino. Two "comfort stations" (restrooms) are on the site as well.

Return to Columbus Drive and walk roughly half the distance between Congress Parkway and Jackson, the next street to the north. On your left, between Columbus Drive and the railroad tracks of the Illinois Central, is:

17. **The Seated Lincoln.** In what was originally planned as a Court of the Presidents, this solitary likeness of Abraham Lincoln has sat alone since 1926. It's the work of the talented, enigmatic American sculptor Augustus Saint-Gaudens.

    Continue north on Columbus and cross East Jackson Drive. Nestled in the northeast corner of this intersection is the:

18. **Petrillo Music Shell.** On evenings in late spring and summer, this single location has traditionally drawn more Chicago residents and visitors to Grant Park than any other attraction. The free outdoor blues (early June) and jazz festivals (around Labor Day) account for vast multitudes of music lovers who crowd into the seats provided or congregate elsewhere on the surrounding grounds. The popular bandshell's fate has been somewhat uncertain with the construction of the new Millennium Park music pavilion (see Stop 2 on this tour).

    Winding Down   Stroll west on Jackson Avenue to visit another Chicago landmark, **Miller's Pub,** 143 S. Wabash Ave. (☎ **312/645-5377**). A favorite with Loop office workers for more than 50 years, Miller's is the perfect spot for a late-afternoon drink and snack (although there's also a full dinner and lunch menu). Check out the walls of celebrity photos (many of them vintage black-and-whites of old-time entertainers) and soak in the timeless atmosphere.

    Walk 1 block north to Monroe Drive, where, in the complex of buildings on your left, we approach our final stop:

19. **The Art Institute of Chicago.** Before walking back to Michigan Avenue along Monroe Street, the first building you come to on Columbus Drive is the School of the Art Institute, including its Betty Rymer Gallery and the Film Center. Also along Columbus Drive, installed in a 1977 addition to the museum, is the Trading Room of the Old Chicago Stock Exchange, a work of Adler and Sullivan, salvaged before the building's demolition. One wag refers to this exhibit as "the Wailing Wall of Chicago's preservationists."

You can enter the museum from this side or go to the main entrance on South Michigan Avenue and Adams Street, at the top of the imposing steps flanked by two formidable bronze lions. As a building, the Art Institute of Chicago is a major Chicago landmark. It was constructed at the time of the World's Columbian Exposition as a venue for conferences for the fair's participants. Today it contains one of the world's great collections of antiquities, paintings, and sculpture. The museum is open Monday to Friday from 10:30am to 4:30pm, Tuesday until 8pm, and Saturday, Sunday, and holidays 10am to 5pm; closed Thanksgiving and December 25. There's a recommended admission fee; the museum is free on Tuesday.

The Magnificent Mile

Start: Michigan Avenue Bridge.

Public Transportation: Take the Red line to the Grand and State subway stop, or bus nos. 145, 146, or 151 to the vicinity of the Chicago River.

Finish: The Drake Hotel, Michigan Avenue and Oak Street.

Time: 1½ to 2 hours; longer if you browse extensively or shop along the way.

Best Time: Daily during normal business hours. Check shops for closing times; many of the vertical malls are open till 7pm or later, except on Sunday. Between Thanksgiving and Christmas, holiday lighting makes the Magnificent Mile a special place to walk after dark.

Worst Time: Whenever the shops or malls are closed.

No section of Chicago reflects the driving changes of the 20th century more than "the

Magnificent Mile," the strip of Michigan Avenue between the Chicago River and Oak Street Beach. The original settlement of Chicago began on the neighborhood's periphery, on the banks of the river, and commercial development spread south for many years.

Most of the earlier 19th-century construction in what is today River North—the North Michigan Avenue area (including Streeterville), the Gold Coast, and Lincoln Park as far north as Fullerton Avenue—did not survive the Chicago Fire. Between 1871 and the mid-1920s, the vast tracts of these contiguous neighborhoods were indistinguishable from the other outlying areas surrounding the downtown Loop. What is today the North Michigan Avenue area was even a bit shabbier than most because of its concentration of cheaply constructed "fire shanties," as much of the temporary post-conflagration housing was dubbed. True, the more daring elements among the city's Mandarin merchant class began to build their mansions in the River North neighborhood and along newly laid out Lake Shore Drive in the 1880s. But between those pockets of isolated splendor and the river bordering downtown, North Michigan Avenue (then called Pine St.) looked more like frontier than metropolis well into the 20th century.

Indeed, the dimensions of the landmass along the lakefront were substantially smaller than they are today. Tons of rubble from the ruins of the fire, plus excess fill from myriad post-fire construction sites, transformed acres of watery frontage east of Pine Street into valuable real estate. While the area's landscape gradually began to change, the large spurt of energy required for full-blown development was slow to materialize. Although Daniel Burnham's 1909 Plan of Chicago laid the conceptual groundwork for creating a wide boulevard to replace Pine Street, not until the 1920s were the engines of urban expansion sufficiently fired.

● ● ● ● ● ● ● ● ● ● ● ● ● ● ● ●

Our tour of North Michigan Avenue—the Magnificent Mile—begins on the opposite bank of the Chicago River, across the:

1. **Michigan Avenue Bridge.** Development of the near north side awaited the construction of a bridge in this location, linking Michigan Avenue below the river to its

new extension above. In 1920, the deed was done. The site anchoring the southern end of the bridge is of deep historical significance. Here, in 1803, Fort Dearborn was erected; at that time it was a major military garrison at the threshold of the Northwest Territory, an area just then opening to settlement for restless citizens from the established states of the new republic. An outline of the original fort is marked on the roadway and in the sidewalk.

The bridge includes several attractions of interest. Don't miss the decorative relief sculptures adorning the pylons: *Defense* and *Regeneration* by Henry Hering to the south, and *The Discoverers* and *The Pioneers* by James Earle Fraser to the north. Like all the spans across the river in downtown Chicago, this is a movable bridge that must open frequently to accommodate a considerable amount of water traffic. The vista from the Michigan Avenue Bridge is particularly fine, taking in a fair stretch of the river skyline to its west—one of the prettiest sights in the city—and opening to a wide view of the lake to its east. The northwest and southwest sides of the bridge are also launch points for several tour boat operators, including the Chicago Architecture Foundation's popular and instructive cruise.

Cross the bridge and stop just beyond the northern end. The distinctive building on the west side of the street, a fitting and monumental gateway to a grand boulevard, is 400 and 410 N. Michigan Ave., the:

2. **William Wrigley Jr. Building.** When this building— actually two buildings side by side—went up, between 1919 and 1924, a trend began in Chicago to match the ever-rising altitude of the New York skyline. The Wrigley family of chewing gum fame continues to own and operate this imposing building. The white terra-cotta cladding covering its facade glitters brightly in the sunlight. In fact, six shades of white distinguish these surface tiles; the darkest tone is at the base, and the colors gradually lighten as the sheathing rises to the roofline. That same brightness reflects beautifully in the water of the nearby river, and is highlighted at night—the prime time to view it— in the glow of innumerable floodlights.

The Magnificent Mile

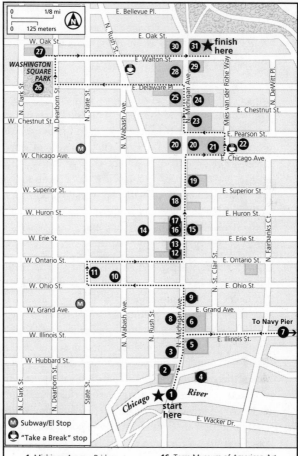

1 Michigan Avenue Bridge
2 William Wrigley Jr. Building
3 Billy Goat Tavern
4 Equitable Building
5 Tribune Tower
6 Hotel Inter-Continental Chicago
7 Navy Pier
8 McGraw-Hill Building
9 543 and 545 North Michigan Avenue
10 Medinah Temple
11 Tree Studios
12 Woman's Athletic Club
13 Crate & Barrel
14 Old McCormick Mansion
15 663 and 669 North Michigan Avenue
16 Terra Museum of American Art
17 City Place
18 Chicago Place
19 Neiman Marcus
20 Chicago Water Tower & Pumping Station
21 Fire House
22 Museum of Contemporary Art
23 Water Tower Place
24 John Hancock Center
25 Fourth Presbyterian Church
26 Washington Square
27 Newberry Library
28 900 North Michigan Avenue
29 Palmolive Building
30 One Magnificent Mile
31 The Drake Hotel

Next look for a stairwell that descends to subterranean Hubbard Street. In the shadowy crevice beneath the concrete walkway at the bottom of the stairs is the:

3. **Billy Goat Tavern.** This short-order dive and tap room is a hangout for newspaper workers from the nearby offices of both the *Chicago Tribune* and the *Chicago Sun-Times.* The official address is 430 N. Michigan Ave. This was the place John Belushi parodied in his classic skit on "Saturday Night Live," a moment in the life of a crabby Greek short-order cook (and yes, they still serve "cheeze-borgers"). "The Goat," incidentally, has a cheap and popular breakfast special, available on weekdays only.

Returning to Michigan Avenue, cross to the east side of the street. Behind the sweeping plaza known as Pioneer Court is 401 N. Michigan Ave., the:

4. **Equitable Building.** When this great slab went up in 1965, Mies van der Rohe was still the rage among urban architects. Many skyscrapers in Chicago derive their inspiration from the philosophy of pure functionalism that the onetime Bauhaus innovator promoted in his later years. The Tribune Company, which occupies the landmark building next door, used to own this property. When the company agreed to part with the prized riverside setting, it included a stipulation that the deep setback, with its wide front yard, be used as public space. That condition makes this otherwise overpowering computer chip of a structure less obtrusive. Part of the plaza's charm is the way it wraps around the building and even leads to a stairway that descends to river level. One block east, behind the Equitable Building, two of Chicago's newest large-scale extravaganzas face each other from opposing corners on Columbus Drive: the **NBC Tower,** designed to look like a building from the 1930s, and the **Sheraton Chicago Hotel and Towers,** a first-class convention establishment.

Together with the Wrigley Building, the grand tower that completes the framing of a postcard composition that has become a visual signature of Chicago is 435 N. Michigan Ave., the:

5. **Tribune Tower.** This is one of Chicago's most interesting structures, because of both its origin and a unique feature that adorns its exterior. In 1922, the *Trib* celebrated its 25th anniversary with a design contest for its new building. Top contenders from around the world weighed in. Among the 264 entries were submissions from Eliel Saarinen (the runner-up) and Walter Gropius. The designs reflected what contemporary architects considered possibilities for the modern skyscraper, though most derived their inspirations from various classical forms of the more or less distant past.

   The firm of John Meade Howells and Raymond M. Hood won the competition and ultimately constructed the winner, a study in gothic, which opened in 1925. The tower stands 36 stories tall and is most distinguished by the sculptured upper stories, which suggest a medieval cathedral. Embedded at various points in the exterior wall are souvenir bits and pieces of historical ruins and monuments, with all origins labeled: the Parthenon, Westminster Abbey, the Taj Mahal, the Alamo, they're all here. The *Tribune*'s founder and its ruling tyrant for many years, Col. Robert R. McCormick, nephew of the great "Reaper" (the inventor Cyrus McCormick), gathered the artifacts. With his trusty international correspondents, McCormick was a master grave robber of the world's treasured antiquities. Another cute feature ornamenting the Trib Tower is the manner in which the two principal architects signed their work: Among the stone carvings decorating a three-story arch that surrounds the entrance are the figures of Robin Hood and a "howling" dog.

   Another historic building at the beginning of the Magnificent Mile lies across Illinois Street. At 505 N. Michigan Ave. is the:

6. **Hotel Inter-Continental Chicago.** This old duck helped ring in the Depression when it was completed in 1929. The elaborate relief panels on three sides of the facade exterior are worth a look. Its art moderne interior was originally home to the Medinah Athletic Club, but it was soon converted into a hotel (a more modern—and undistinguished—addition was tacked on a few decades

later). The building recently underwent a massive renovation; it now holds first-class hotel accommodations. While the new, remodeled lobby is somewhat sterile, take a look inside the entrance closest to Illinois Street for a taste of the original hotel's grandeur, albeit in miniature.

Our next stop requires a diversion from Michigan Avenue. You may wish to detour now, or perhaps follow another day. If you're ready, descend the stairs to Illinois and walk toward the lake (or catch one of the free trolley shuttles). You'll come to:

7. **Navy Pier,** about a half mile due east. Built as a municipal pier during World War I, Navy Pier has a colorful history as an entertainment center, a freight and passenger terminal, a training center for Navy pilots during World War II, and a satellite campus of the University of Illinois. In 1995 it underwent a long-anticipated transformation that has returned it, at least in spirit, to its original intended purpose. Today it's a place for Chicagoans (or rather suburbanites and tourists) to relax and be entertained. Developers resurrected the Grand Ballroom and installed the Crystal Gardens, which hold 70 full-size palm trees, dancing fountains, and other flora in a glass-enclosed atrium. Also here is the white-canopied, open-air Skyline Stage, which schedules concerts, dance performances, and film screenings; a carousel; and a 15-story Ferris wheel that's a replica of the original from Chicago's 1893 world's fair. The 50 acres of pier and lakefront property also are home to the Chicago Shakespeare Theater, Chicago Children's Museum, a 3-D Imax theater, and a small ice rink. There are a handful of shops and pushcart vendors, several restaurants, and a beer garden with live music. There's definitely something for everyone, and the spectacular view of the city from the end of the 3,000-foot pier is worth the walk.

After your detour to Navy Pier, return on Illinois Street to Michigan Avenue. Once the sleepier end of the street, the area toward the bridge was energized in 2000 with the opening of a Nordstorm department store and a glitzy new mall. Don't overlook an integral part of the huge new development known as North Bridge, the:

8. **McGraw-Hill Building,** 520 N. Michigan Ave., with Hugo Boss and a few other boutiques on its ground floor. This landmark building isn't what it seems. The 1921 structure was sacrificed somewhat to make room for the new retail and hotel project. Workers took down the Art Deco facade slab by slab; the original building was demolished; and the original building skin was attached to a new steel skeleton. The exterior incorporates wonderful decorative friezes of astrological signs by Gwen Lux, who later did work at Rockefeller Center in New York City. Four of the panels are displayed inside the mall entrance, behind the concierge desk. The procedure, known as a "facadectomy," had never been done before on such a tall building, but it rankled many preservationists who disapprove of messing with the integrity of a building. While the McGraw-Hill Building isn't a stunner, it still represents a glimpse at what this boulevard looked like before the towering megamalls transformed it into the retail extravaganza it is today.

Cross the street to the east side of the avenue for a visit to:

9. **543 and 545 N. Michigan Ave.** Today housing a Timberland apparel store, this mildly Art Deco building provides a more accurate profile of the scale of Michigan Avenue as it appeared during the 1920s than do the Wrigley Building and the Tribune Tower. The building's mansard roof reflects the French training of architect Phillip B. Maher, and the reliefs of female figures above the entry recall the days when a *salon d'haute couture* occupied the original storefront.

A slight digression 2 blocks west along Ohio Street to 600 N. Wabash brings you to the subject of a recent historic preservation battle, the:

10. **Medinah Temple.** This fanciful Moorish palace was the regional headquarters of the Shriners and site of their highly regarded annual circus. You'll have to imagine the building's pair of patinaed onion domes, which were so distressed that they had to be removed several years ago. The Shriners have since sold the building, which was nearly ruined in an ill-considered development plan.

Public outcry led to a sympathetic developer's taking over the site, with plans to restore the temple's exterior and some of the highlights of the interior before turning it into the new home of a Bloomingdale's furniture store.

Walk around the block to see another vestige of the neighborhood's roots, the:

11. **Tree Studios,** 601–623 N. State St. Built in 1894 (and expanded in the teens) to encourage visiting artists working on the world's fair to stay in Chicago, this row of cottage-like buildings was built with retail stores on street level and artists' studios upstairs, and continues in that tradition today. Plans also call for it to be saved as part of a redevelopment of the entire block.

   Ohio Street is a gateway to the theme park–style restaurant zone that has sprung up in recent years on this end of River North, the neighborhood immediately west of the Magnificent Mile. (See *Frommer's Chicago* for full restaurant listings.)

   Walk up to Ontario, turn right, and return to Michigan Avenue. On the corner of Ontario Street at 626 N. Michigan Ave. is the:

12. **Woman's Athletic Club.** The style and grace of this Phillip B. Maher creation, built in 1928, recalls an era of transatlantic steamship lines and "putting on the Ritz." You can almost imagine this building having been imported stone by stone directly from Paris, where its many models and predecessors reside to this day.

   Continuing up the street, at 646 N. Michigan Ave. is:

13. **Crate & Barrel.** This attractive, ultramodern retail space is one of the few new developments along the Magnificent Mile that pays respect to the scale and elegance of the late 1920s, when three-, four-, and five-story buildings dominated the immediate skyline. Householders beware: There's some mighty attractive "stuff" in this store. For a great view of the bustling Michigan Avenue crowds, head up to the top floor and stand out on the balcony overlooking the street.

   Turning left onto Erie Street and walking west for a block or two, you can get some notion of what old River North looked like. On the periphery of Pine Street during the 1880s, the wealthy built mansions on the ruins of immigrant houses after the Great Fire. First is the:

14. **Old McCormick Mansion.** The entrance is on North Rush Street at no. 660. This old manse (1875), one of several family residences remaining from when this area was known as "McCormickville," was the home of Cyrus McCormick's brother. Behind the roofline of an addition, you can make out a fragment of the splendid palazzo that belonged to L. Hamilton McCormick, another beneficiary of Cyrus's good fortune.

On the next corner, at Wabash, is 40 E. Erie St. Another period mansion (1883), the former home of Samuel M. Nickerson today houses the R. H. Love Galleries.

Back on Michigan Avenue, turn your attention to:

15. **663 and 669 N. Michigan Ave.** Vintage buildings like this one have been razed elsewhere along Michigan Avenue by developers putting up modern mega-projects. But creative recycling of this 1920s structure, the former home of Saks Fifth Avenue, has only added to one of the most successful retail spaces in Chicago. Two flagship shops, **Niketown** and the **Sony Gallery of Consumer Electronics,** occupy adjoining buildings. You must enter them to appreciate their innovations in interior decor and layout. The Nike store is a three-story pavilion, divided into various sports environments. The less glitzy Sony store is more of a hands-on showcase than an outlet for the endless stream of electronic gadgets from Japan.

Across the boulevard, at 666 N. Michigan Ave., is the home of one of the more interesting art collections in the city, the:

16. **Terra Museum of American Art.** The focus is work created in the 18th, 19th, and 20th centuries. What began as the private collection of industrialist Daniel J. Terra now comprises more than 400 unique pieces spread over many galleries. The museum is free on Tuesdays.

One of the more visually daring structures among Chicago's most recent crop of skyscrapers is at 676 N. Michigan Ave.:

17. **City Place,** built in 1990. The curvy, futuristic design running the height of the facade looks like the upright panel of a giant pinball machine; you'll either find it very attractive or, as one critic called it, "garish." The Omni Hotel Chicago occupies the middle floors of the multiuse high rise.

    Across Huron Street is another behemoth, 700 N. Michigan Ave., or:

18. **Chicago Place.** Saks Fifth Avenue is the flagship of Chicago's most recently inaugurated retail skyscraper (1991). Some 50 shops and stores, wrapped around an atrium, rise eight stories from street level to a food court bathed in natural light and surrounded by potted greenery.

    The spirit of Texan exaggeration animates our next stop, at 737 N. Michigan Ave. It's the First Church of Upward Mobility, otherwise known as:

19. **Neiman Marcus.** As commercial theater at its most fantastic, no one does it on a grander scale. The four-story lobby, trimmed in marble and brass and centered on a soaring, curved wooden sculpture, is definitely worth a stop for a few moments of gawking and jaw dropping. This multiuse complex—the store (1983) and the high-altitude **Olympia Center** (1986) around the corner at 161 E. Chicago—is the work of Skidmore, Owings & Merrill. It pays homage in a variety of design and decorative features to the styles of Louis Sullivan and H. H. Richardson.

    Across Chicago Avenue, on either side of Michigan Avenue, are two structures that lay undisputed claim to the status of First Landmark of Chicago, the:

20. **Chicago Water Tower and Pumping Station.** Two years after their construction in 1869, the path of the Chicago Fire swept away virtually every building in the vicinity. But the Water Tower and Pumping Station survived unscathed. Fate decrees its choices with a certain irony; why, many wags have wondered over the years, was so much surrounding beauty reduced to ashes while these two beasts were allowed to stand? One wit suggested that both buildings look as if they belong at the bottom of a

fish tank, and indeed they do appear for all the world like mutant sand castles left behind from the set of some made-for-TV sci-fi melodrama.

The castellated style, here practiced by the accomplished Chicago architect William W. Boyington in the medium of yellow-tinted Illinois limestone, was wildly popular in its day. And whatever one's aesthetic judgment about the value of the architecture—on three occasions in the past 90 years, the tower narrowly escaped demolition—the Water Tower's importance as a symbol of Chicago's survival cannot be underestimated. A restoration campaign begun in 1962 finally gave public recognition to that fact. A city art gallery has opened in the Water Tower, which is now at the center of a newly landscaped park based on designs by Victor Skrebneski, the internationally known fashion photographer who makes Chicago his home. On the premises of the old Pumping Station are a Visitor's Center staffed by the Chicago Office of Tourism, a cafe, and the home of one of the city's most adventurous mid-size theaters, Lookingglass Theatre.

Turn right and walk east on Chicago Avenue. At no. 202 East, notice the:

21. **Fire House.** The base for Engine Co. 98, this is one of the oldest fire houses in the city. Operating since 1904, it was built in imitation of the castellated gothic style of the Water Tower and Pumping Station. When was the last time you saw stained-glass windows and a dark-stained wood ceiling in a fire station?

Tiny 1-acre Seneca Park, with its Eli Schulman Playground, is directly east. Eli Schulman was a Chicago restaurateur and philanthropist whose famous steak house, Eli's, is just across the street.

Take a Break Eli's . . . **The Place for Steak,** 215 E. Chicago Ave. (☎ 312/642-1393), is famous for cheesecake, making the restaurant the perfect spot for a midmorning or midafternoon coffee break. There are 50 varieties of cheesecake from which to choose (try the turtle cheesecake for a real sugar rush). On a sunny day, bask on the terrace at the Museum of Contemporary Art (see below) at **Puck's,** a cafe named for celebrity chef Wolfgang Puck that overlooks the museum's sculpture garden. The menu incorporates Mediterranean and Asian influences, including many signature items from Puck's restaurant Spago (which has an outpost in Chicago). There's both an express counter and table service; museum admission is not required for dining.

Across the small street named for Mies van der Rohe, at 220 E. Chicago Ave., is the prominent new site of the:

22. **Museum of Contemporary Art,** which opened here to great fanfare during a 24-hour summer solstice celebration in 1996. (The museum reprises the party each year around the first day of summer with another round-the-clock open house.) The rather somber-looking museum, designed by Josef Paul Kleihues of Berlin (his first American project), pays homage to Mies van der Rohe, Louis Sullivan, and other great Chicago architects. The MCA emphasizes experimentation in a variety of media—painting, photography, video, dance, music, and performance. Exhibits change frequently, and the MCA also has a permanent collection, especially strong in works by Chicago artists.

Now cross over to Pearson Street along Mies van der Rohe Way. The palazzo on the northeast corner of the intersection (200 E. Pearson St.) was the residence of the renowned architect for whom the street is named. Mies, according to local lore, had free digs in the complex he designed on nearby Lake Shore Drive, but he had to flee. Every time the tenants had a maintenance problem, they called on the architect, as if he were the building's super.

Turn left on Pearson Street and walk back toward Michigan Avenue. The massive marble block-sized building between Pearson Street and Chestnut, directly across from the Pumping Station at 845 N. Michigan Ave., is:

23. **Water Tower Place.** This is the mother of all Chicago vertical malls, built in 1976. When Marshall Field and Company, Chicago's most popular homegrown department store, opened this "uptown" branch, many city denizens no longer had a reason to visit State Street, the traditional center of retailing in the Loop, where the

original Marshall Field's remains. Among the other high-toned occupants of Water Tower Place are Lord & Taylor and the 431-room Ritz-Carlton Hotel, spread over 22 floors.

☕ **Take a Break** The concept may sound like your standard food court, but **foodlife** (☎ 312/335-FOOD) is a healthier, more creative version. Located on the mezzanine level of Water Tower Place, it offers dishes from a dozen different stands in a cozy, plant-filled setting. You have your pick of everything from pizza and sandwiches to Asian, Italian and Mexican specialities, all made fresh. If you're traveling with a group, you'll find something here to please everyone.

On the next block north, at 875 N. Michigan Ave., stands a 100-story building that is only the third-tallest structure in Chicagoland, the:

24. **John Hancock Center.** "Big John" (1969) was the first real giant to appear on the skyline, inaugurating a trend toward high-altitude construction in downtown Chicago. New Yorkers in particular were outraged when Chicago dared to raise a building that eclipsed their revered Empire State, for many years the tallest building in the world. But Big John's claim to that distinction was short-lived, as construction companies in Chicago, Toronto, New York, and even Kuala Lumpur began a game of high-rise one-upmanship.

In Chicago, however, Big John has not been forgotten; among architects and engineers in particular, the building retains a strong following. The tech-heads speak highly of the building's structural innovations, the crisscross steel framing, the tapering form that suggests a monument of super proportions, and the neat little fact that certain engineering breakthroughs kept the cost down to that of a building half its height. An observatory on the 94th floor is open to the public, as is a bar and restaurant duplex between the 95th and 96th floors. New additions to the lower levels of the building include an attractive elliptical plaza and several retailers. At the Chicago Architecture Foundation store, you can browse through the books and gift items and inquire about the group's guided tours.

Streeterville

The area around the John Hancock Center, east to the lake and north to Oak Street, bordering North Michigan Avenue, is known as Streeterville. Behind the colorful name is a colorful tale. In 1896, George Wellington "Cap" Streeter, a circus showman, ran his leaky scow aground in the shallows near what is today Chicago Avenue. After several weeks, when the tides refused to free the stranded craft, Cap Streeter dug in for the duration. First he built a narrow causeway, spanning the swampy wetland between his boat and the shoreline. Next, he invited local builders to dump their fill near his involuntary abode.

In a short time, Streeter was surrounded by 150 acres of prime real estate in a neighborhood undergoing a period of rapid development. Because the landmass did not appear on the map of the Illinois shoreline survey, Streeter claimed it for the federal government and appointed himself territorial governor. When Streeter started trying to sell off his holdings, the city of Chicago finally tired of the antics of the man the local papers dubbed the "Squatter King." The city took Streeter to court, but it was not until 1918 that an order was issued for his eviction—not for squatting on city land, but for violating the municipal blue laws by selling spirits on Sundays. Cap Streeter's tenancy in his landfill "federal district" had lasted over 20 years, and it is only fitting that today the area he helped create bears his name.

Across from Big John, at 866 N. Michigan Ave., is:

25. **Fourth Presbyterian Church (1914).** This splendid gothic creation is by Ralph Adams Cram and parishioner Howard Van Doren Shaw. With its cloistered courtyard, illuminated ceiling, and saintly statuary, it is much closer to the Roman tradition than to the plain-wrapper meeting houses favored by simpler folk since the days of the Reformation.

For those who would like to visit the oldest park in Chicago, I recommend a brief detour off the Magnificent Mile, several blocks west along Delaware to Dearborn. Along the way, at 15 W. Delaware Place, you'll pass the first new synagogue built in the central city in 30 years. Founded in 1861 and recently located in Hyde Park, Chicago Sinai Congregation opened its striking new limestone-clad building in 1997.

Take a Break A sleek spot for a lunch or quick bite is **Zoom Kitchen,** 923 N. Rush St. (☎ **312/ 440-3500**), a walk-through cafe that prepares everything to order. Options include carved meats, salads made before your eyes, homemade soups, and comfort foods like mashed potatoes and spicy macaroni and cheese. If you have kids in tow, they may feel more at home across the street at **Johnny Rockets,** a retro 1950s-style diner.

Continue on Delaware another block to:

26. **Washington Square.** This is Chicago's famous Bughouse Square, described in James T. Farrell's *Studs Lonigan* trilogy. In this "outdoor forum of garrulous hobohemia," an oddball collection of soap-box orators, expounding on anything from free love to a stateless society, harangued each other and crowds of derisive, delighted onlookers throughout the 1920s.

    Surrounding Washington Square are some fine old mansions, renovated town houses, and new apartment buildings. The granite fortress across the street at 60 W. Walton St. is the glorious:

27. **Newberry Library.** The Newberry was established in 1887 and is a researcher's paradise, particularly for those involved with European and American studies. Included in the collection are 1.5 million volumes, among them many rarities; more than 5 million manuscripts; and 75,000 maps. Many interesting artifacts are displayed in free public exhibitions, and the library itself is open, if you apply for a reader's card. The institution was the bequest of Chicago financier and merchant Walter Loomis Newberry, and the building the work of architect

Henry Ives Cobb. In the late 1990s the building got a once-in-a-century scrubbing that scraped off decades of soot and grime. Most Chicagoans were surprised to learn that the library was built not of dark piles of stone but of creamy pink granite!

Return to Michigan Avenue along Walton Street. On the southwest corner of Michigan and Walton is:

28. **900 N. Michigan Ave.** The most upscale of the Magnificent Mile's high-rise malls, this is known locally as the Bloomingdale's building. Crammed with fine specialty shops around a central atrium, 900 N. Michigan Ave. feels somewhat sterile but attracts a well-heeled crowd (which is no surprise, considering its tenants include Gucci, Max Mara, and other pricey clothing lines). However, it's also home to a number of reasonably priced restaurants.

For the last three points of interest, we will crisscross Michigan Avenue several times. Directly across from Bloomingdale's at 919 N. Michigan Ave. is the original:

29. **Palmolive Building.** For years this 1929 vintage study in Art Deco was called the Playboy Building, during the era when the skin-mag giant held sway here (it's now at 680 N. Lake Shore Dr.). With the knockout views from the upper floors, it's no surprise that the building has been redeveloped as luxury condos.

The building at 940–980 N. Michigan Ave., on the corner of Oak Street, is known as:

30. **One Magnificent Mile.** A main attraction here is Spiaggia, one of Chicago's most consistently popular Italian restaurants since the mid-1980s. If your dogs aren't barking by now (and if you left your credit cards back in your hotel room), you may want to take another detour down Oak Street. The small powerhouse of a block is home to small fashion boutiques, upscale home decor stores, and a few big names (Barneys New York, Prada).

Our tour of North Michigan Avenue appropriately draws to a close at the building across from One Magnificent Mile, with its entrance at 140 E. Walton St.:

31. **The Drake Hotel.** Built in 1920 by Marshall & Fox, the Drake has maintained a consistent level of fine service and luxury accommodations for more than 70 years. The 13-story building is a Chicago landmark, constructed of Bedford limestone in a design inspired by the Italian palazzi of the late Renaissance. A stroll through the lobby, especially the serene and tasteful Palm Court, is definitely worthwhile. With its privileged view of the lakefront, the Drake stands at the transition point between downtown Chicago and the elegant residential neighborhood called the Gold Coast.

The Gold Coast

Start: East Lake Shore Drive, across from the Oak Street Beach (behind the Drake Hotel).

Public Transportation: Your best bet is the no. 145, 146 or 151 Michigan Avenue bus; get off between Walton and Oak streets. Or take the Red line subway to Chicago and State; walk east a couple of blocks to Michigan, and then north to Oak Street.

Finish: Bellevue Place and Michigan Avenue.

Time: 2 hours.

Best Times: Sunday is the ideal day for this walk at any time of year. On weekdays, before or after the morning rush, the streets are empty enough for you to enjoy unjostled solitude. On a bright day, set out when the sun is low in the sky and casts flat and even light.

Worst Times: Whenever crowded beaches or streets make the walk heavy going.

T he Gold Coast is the silk-stocking district of Chicago. It is small and exclusive, as you might expect of a neighborhood that contains some of the world's most valuable real estate. The bulk of the neighborhood lies between Oak Street and Lincoln Park, bounded on the east by Lake Shore Drive, with LaSalle Street above

Division forming the western margin between the Gold Coast and Old Town.

Until the 1880s, this land was largely vacant, with some sections serving as burial grounds (later condemned as "unhealthy"). The State Street merchant Potter Palmer broke with the norm; instead of building his mansion south of the Loop around Prairie Avenue (where many giants of industry and commerce had their homes), he went north. In 1882, Palmer built a lakeshore castle bordering marshlands in what was then a relative wilderness. This prince of Chicago retailing reportedly had a speculative scheme in mind when he chose this area. And indeed, the mere presence of the Palmers, then one of the most prominent families in Chicago society, served as an instant magnet, drawing the carriage trade north in droves. The value of Palmer's extensive north-side holdings escalated rapidly, as the price of land rose 400 percent in a few short years. Whether wittingly or by chance, Potter Palmer had spun his marsh grass into gold.

Our itinerary combines a leisurely stroll on Chicago's downtown strand along Lake Michigan with a walk among the fine town houses that line the tree-shaded interior streets of the Gold Coast.

● ● ● ● ● ● ● ● ● ● ● ● ● ● ● ● ●

Take the underpass beneath Michigan Avenue to reach the:

1. **Oak Street Beach.** Enjoy the luxury of a walk in the sand smack in the middle of downtown Chicago; it may not be Copacabana, but neither New York nor Los Angeles can claim such a bonny downtown amenity. If the sand doesn't suit you, stick to the concrete path, making sure to stay alert to avoid being run down by a speeding bicyclist or blader. On your right is the sweeping vista of the great inland waterway, Lake Michigan. At some distance, you are almost certain to see signs of the stolid commercial shipping that plies these waters, as vessels crawl along the horizon. While you're ambling, there's nothing to prevent you from admiring the residential behemoths on the opposite side of Lake Shore Drive. (Or you may choose to follow the pedestrian tunnel under the

drive at Division St. for a closer inspection.) Among the giant structures, take note also of the few remaining mansions, the relics of a gilded age.

Beginning just above Scott Street, you will see a cluster of four such exemplars of that privileged past, including the:

2. **Carl C. Heissen House,** 1250 Lake Shore Dr. Also nearby stand the Mason Brayman Starring House, at no. 1254; the Arthur T. Aldis House, at no. 1258; and the Lawrence D. Rockwell House, at no. 1260. Both the Heissen House (1890) and its immediate neighbor, the Starring House (1889), strongly suggest the long-standing affection of wealthy Chicagoans for the sturdy Romanesque, which soon thereafter gave way to the lighter continental lines of the Second Empire.

A second cluster of former private mansions, all vaguely neoclassical in outline and appointments, faces Lake Michigan toward the north end of this stretch of the boardwalk, beginning at:

3. **1516 N. Lake Shore Dr.** This building is home to the International College of Surgeons; its neighbor at no. 1524 is a museum belonging to the same institution. The International Museum of Surgical Science houses a fascinating collection of exhibits and artifacts that portray the evolution of medical surgery. Chicago architect Howard Van Doren Shaw designed the museum building in 1917 as a private mansion. Another reason for entering the museum (besides the collection) is to view the well-preserved interior of Shaw's creation, including the massive stone staircase and the second-floor library, with its fine wood paneling. A third structure, 1530 N. Lake Shore Dr., a creation of Benjamin Marshall, is today the Polish Consulate.

This stroll along the water should take between 15 and 30 minutes. If you have been following the inland side of Lake Shore Drive, cross back to the park using the North Avenue underpass. Follow the path to the Chess Pavilion on your left, and continue past the patch of green where the jetty leads out to a harbor light and into the parking lot. Straight on is the:

The Gold Coast

1 Oak Street Beach
2 Carl C. Heissen House
3 1516 North Lake Shore Drive
4 North Avenue Beach
5 Residence of the Roman Catholic
  Archbishop of Chicago
6 1550 North State Parkway
7 Bullock Folsom House
8 4 West Burton Place
9 Cyrus H. McCormick Mansion
10 1525 North Astor Street
11 1451 and 1449 North Astor Street
12 1443 and 1444 North Astor Street
13 1427 North Astor Street
14 1421 North Astor Street
15 1416 North Astor Street
16 Thomas W. Hinde House
17 Joseph T. Ryerson House
18 Charnley-Persky House
19 Astor Court
20 Playboy Mansion
21 1328 North State Parkway
22 James L. Houghteling houses
23 1301 and 1260 North Astor Street
24 Renaissance Condominiums
25 East Cedar Street
26 Lot P. Smith House
27 Fortnightly of Chicago

4. **North Avenue Beach.** This is the next strand up the line, on the southern end of Lincoln Park. The beach house playfully resembles an old ocean liner. The upper deck has a grill and bar with terrific views, and the beach below is a mecca for sandlot volleyball enthusiasts.

Now double back and cross Lake Shore Drive by way of the North Avenue underpass, directly west of the Chess Pavilion. From the cul-de-sac here, continue west on North Avenue 2 blocks to North State Parkway. The imposing residence on your left, surrounded by spacious grounds, is the:

5. **Residence of the Roman Catholic Archbishop of Chicago.** The estate's official address is 1555 N. State Pkwy. This mansion (1880) is an example in red brick of early Queen Anne styling. Archbishop Patrick Feehan was the first resident of the mansion, which stands on the former grounds of a cemetery that stretched between present-day North Avenue and Schiller Street. By the turn of the century, the Chicago Archdiocese had subdivided much of this remaining Gold Coast property, providing house sites for many affluent families. A virtual battalion of chimney pots marches across the roofline of this old episcopal residence, which is one of the oldest and most familiar on the Gold Coast.

Across the street on the opposite corner of North Avenue is:

6. **1550 N. State Pkwy.** Each apartment in this 1912 vintage luxury high-rise, known locally as the Benjamin Marshall Building, originally occupied a single floor and contained 15 rooms spread over 9,000 square feet. The architects were Marshall & Fox, highly regarded in their day as builders of fine hotels. There was once a garden entryway at the ground-floor level. Among the noteworthy architectural features adorning the exterior of this beaux arts classic are the many small balconies and the bowed windows at the corners of the building.

Continue west for 1 block on North Avenue and turn left, following Dearborn Street to Burton Place and the:

7. **Bullock Folsom House.** As its mansard roof reveals, this landmark 1877 home on the southwest corner, at

1454 N. Dearborn St., is pure Second Empire. That roof, incidentally, is shingled in slate, not asphalt. Neighboring houses at nos. 1450 and 1434 have some of the same French-influenced ornamentation and styling. Across Burton Place just to the north, at 1500 N. Dearborn St., is another example of a rival architectural fashion of the day, the Richardsonian or Romanesque Revival.

Now return to the east along Burton, but before crossing North State Parkway, stop at:

8. **4 W. Burton Place.** Built as a private residence in 1902 by Richard E. Schmidt for a family named Madlener, this striking continental structure today houses the Graham Foundation for Advanced Studies in the Fine Arts. There is something very modern about the appearance of this former home; the clean, sleek lines of its ornamentation seem to foreshadow the Art Deco styling still 2 decades off.

Now continue 1 block farther east to Astor Street. On the northwest corner, at 1500 N. Astor St., is the former:

9. **Cyrus H. McCormick Mansion.** New York architect Stanford White designed this building, which was constructed for the Patterson family in 1893. Cyrus McCormick, Jr., bought it in 1914, and David Adler's north addition doubled the size of the building in 1927. Like so many of New York's Fifth Avenue mansions (also influenced by White and his contemporaries), the McCormick palazzo is an essay in the neoclassical. Square and grand, like a temple of antiquity, the construction combines Roman bricks of burnt yellow with touches of terra-cotta trim. The building has been divided into condominiums.

The tour loops north briefly on Astor Street to take in a home of historical interest:

10. **1525 N. Astor St.** This attractive town house was once the residence of Robert Todd Lincoln, the only surviving child of Abraham and Mary Todd Lincoln. The younger Lincoln took up the private practice of law in Chicago after the Civil War. He remained in Chicago for much of his life, leaving twice during the 1880s and 1890s,

to serve under presidents James Garfield and Chester A. Arthur as Secretary of War, and later under Benjamin Harrison as minister to Britain. On the death of George Pullman, one of his major corporate clients, Lincoln assumed the presidency of the Pullman Palace Car Company in 1897.

Reversing direction again, walk south along Astor Street. Notice the houses at:

11. **1451 and 1449 N. Astor St.** The former, occupying the corner lot, is the work of Howard Van Doren Shaw, built in 1910 according to the so-called Jacobethan fashion. This obscure term combines the words "Jacobean" and "Elizabethan." It describes a revival form of certain 16th- and 17th-century features of English architecture, including narrow, elongated windows, split-level roofs, and multiple chimney stacks. The house at no. 1449 was built around the turn of the century, but the architect of this glorious château remains a mystery. Guarding the home's entrance is a somewhat intimidating stone porch, seemingly out of scale. Among the home's other unique characteristics are the big front bay and the frieze below the cornice, a scroll of stylized shells.

Two other neighboring homes of interest, facing each other across the street, are:

12. **1443 and 1444 N. Astor St.** According to one Chicago author, the May House at no. 1443 "bears a resemblance to H. H. Richardson's Glessner House," the historic landmark south of the Loop at 1800 S. Prairie Ave. Across Astor Street is no. 1444, a true sampler of the Chicago Art Deco style, built in 1929 by Holabird & Roche. Next, walk to:

13. **1427 N. Astor St.** The dean of Chicago architects and pioneer of the earliest skyscrapers, William Le Baron Jenny, designed this structure in 1889. A few years ago this home was on the market for $3 million. Many neighboring homes are valued in this range (give or take a million). This will give you some idea of why they call this neighborhood the Gold Coast.

Several doors down is:

The McCormicks of Chicago

Cyrus H. McCormick Jr. was the son of the man credited with the invention of the reaper, perhaps the single most important mechanical advancement of its day in agriculture. The reaper made it possible to farm huge tracts of wheat on the fertile prairie without depending on seasonal labor for its harvest. The senior McCormick, a native of Virginia, built his first factory in Chicago in 1847. Wiped out by the fire of 1871, the McCormicks were able to rebuild easily. The demand for the company's farm implements was firmly established, and the family fortune already made several times over.

So many members of the McCormick family once occupied homes near Rush and Erie streets, just south of the Gold Coast, that the neighborhood was known as "McCormicksville." Cyrus Jr. became the first president of International Harvester when the McCormick Harvesting Company merged with several of its former competitors in 1902. The McCormicks were no friends of the working class; their plant was an ongoing target of labor agitation during the 1880s. A rally at the McCormick plant in 1886, during which police killed a worker, fueled the infamous Haymarket affair on the following night.

14. **1421 N. Astor St.** This somewhat fanciful but appealing "cottage" was once the base in Chicago of a Catholic missionary order, the Maryknoll Fathers.

    Across the street is:

15. **1416 N. Astor St.** This was another Gold Coast residence belonging to the McCormick clan.

    The neighboring structure at 1412 N. Astor St. is the:

16. **Thomas W. Hinde House.** This 1892 home, created by Douglas S. Pentecost, is a study in the Flemish architecture of the late Middle Ages. The facade has been altered, but some of the original stone ornamentation

remains, as do such dominant features as the multipaned, diamond-shaped windows.

On the same side of the street at 1406 N. Astor St. is the:

17. **Joseph T. Ryerson House.** David Adler designed this 1922 landmark home in the manner of a Parisian hotel; it evokes the scale and delicacy of the buildings that to this day line Left Bank streets. Adler himself supervised the 1931 addition of the top floor and the mansard roof. Woven into the wrought-iron grillwork above the entrance are the initials of the original owner.

The next house to warrant our attention is also a landmark, one that incarnates the collaborative genius of three giants of American architecture. At 1365 N. Astor St., on the southeast corner of Schiller Street, stands the:

18. **Charnley-Persky House.** Shortly before he left the firm of Adler and Sullivan, a then-obscure draftsman, Frank Lloyd Wright, played a major role in designing this 1892 home. The house seems suitable to our modern world, though it's in this fairyland neighborhood where most residences have borrowed their shapes and forms from antiquity. This is either because Wright was so in tune with the special needs of the American domestic landscape, or because there is something timeless, even universal, in his ideas. The **Society of Architectural Historians** (☎ 312/915-0105) gives tours on Wednesday and Saturday. Charles Persky donated the building to the society in 1995.

Continuing down the block, pause before 1355 N. Astor St., known as:

19. **Astor Court.** Row houses are not common in spacious Chicago, so this multiple unit is rare on that account. It's also noteworthy as a window on Georgian formality, which is much more characteristic of parts of London. Because of the ornament above the central drive, which leads to a formal inner court surrounded by residential units, the building is sometimes referred to by its nickname, "The Court of the Golden Hands."

Now walk back to Schiller Street. Cross the street and turn left on North State Parkway, continuing south until roughly the middle of the block, where you'll come to the:

20. **Playboy Mansion.** This bulky mansion at 1340 N. State Pkwy. was built in 1899 for an upright Calvinist named George S. Isham. Although *Playboy*'s Hugh Hefner lived here during his Chicago heyday, the place, now condos, still has the whiff of the countinghouse about it. Here old Hugh romped with his bunnies, the commodities around which he made his fortune, and perfected the airbrushed version of erotica and cracker-barrel hedonism that once made him the nation's reigning purveyor of soft-core porn.

     Continue south on State. A renowned contemporary architect had his hand in our next stop:

21. **1328 N. State Pkwy.** Bertrand Goldberg, who was responsible for Marina City—the corncob-like mixed residential, commercial, nautical towers across from the Loop on the Chicago River—remodeled two separate homes into this property. The 1938 vintage dwellings were connected in 1956 to serve as studio and home for Goldberg's mother-in-law, sculptor Lillian Florsheim.

     Our tour now swings one block east, back to Astor Street by way of Goethe Street. Turn left, and at 1308–1312 N. Astor St. look at the:

22. **James L. Houghteling Houses.** Here's an eclectic cluster of town houses built by Burnham and Root between 1887 and 1888. Originally there were four dwellings, but no. 1306 was torn down. John Wellborn Root, who is credited with the design of the buildings, lived with his family in no. 1310. Here the brilliant architect died of pneumonia at the age of 40.

     On opposite corners diagonally across Goethe Street are apartment towers that represent the trend toward high-rise living on the interior streets of the Gold Coast, which began in the 1930s:

23. **1301 and 1260 N. Astor St.** Constructed by Philip B. Maher in 1932 and 1931, respectively, these apartment buildings are classics of the sleek modernism that characterized American commercial architecture after World War I. At 1300 N. Astor St. is a 1960s version of the high-rise apartment house, by Bertrand Goldberg, in a form that seemed avant-garde in that period (like the fins on Detroit gas guzzlers) and today seems dated.

Now we get a chance to stretch our legs a bit on this quiet lanelike street, which seems protected behind the wall of towering condominiums on Lake Shore Drive. Walk 2 blocks south on Astor Street to the corner of Division Street. The old building on the right is the:

24. **Renaissance Condominiums.** The address is 1210 N. Astor St.; the building, a Holabird & Roche design, dates from 1897. This is one of the rare examples of a Chicago School building on the north side. Notice its similarity in construction to the buildings of the same vintage that remain in the Loop along Dearborn Street, especially the brickwork and the window bays.

Turn right on Division Street.

Take a Break If you need sustenance, continue two blocks to Dearborn Street, turn north, and walk to the **Third Coast,** 1260 N. Dearborn (☎ 312/649-0730), below street level. This cozy coffeehouse has a devoted neighborhood following and is practically always open (until 3am most nights, 24 hr. on summer weekends). On a brisk fall day, it's an ideal spot for a cup of soup and a sandwich.

Return to Division Street and walk 1 block east to State Street. Turn right, staying on the east side of the street where State and Rush merge, and proceed 2 blocks south to:

25. **East Cedar Street.** This long block between Rush Street and Lake Shore Drive deserves a look, because much of its turn-of-the-century scale has been so well preserved. Some of the homes of later vintage are unique and elegant. See in particular the two clusters of "cottages," nos. 42–48 (1896) and 50–54 (1892). These homes illustrate the once-widespread popularity in Chicago of the Romanesque Revival style in domestic architecture. State Street merchant prince Potter Palmer built the first group.

Return now to Rush Street, walk to the next block south, and turn left on Bellevue Place. At 32 E. Bellevue Place stands the:

26. **Lot P. Smith House.** It took a certain kind of chutzpah, even in 1887 when this delightful place was built, to name your child "Lot." In any event, this Lot had both the righteous good fortune and the good sense to have had his home designed by John Wellborn Root.

   At the end of the block, not far from Lake Shore Drive, is our final stop in the Gold Coast: 120 E. Bellevue Place, the:

27. **Fortnightly of Chicago.** New York architect Charles F. McKim, a partner of Stanford White's, built this mansion while sojourning in Chicago as a lead designer of the World's Columbian Exposition. It helped introduce the Georgian fashion in architecture that would replace the Romanesque Revival throughout the Gold Coast. A woman's social club has occupied the premises since 1922.

   Winding Down Another venerable Chicago hotel, the **Drake** (☎ **312/787-2200**), offers the perfect haven for post-walking-tour refreshment—afternoon tea or cocktails in the swank surroundings of the Palm Court, or a sandwich and ice cream in the Oak Terrace. Just continue down Bellevue Place to Lake Shore Drive and cross to the hotel entrance, 2 short blocks south at Walton Street.

Old Town

Start: The southwest corner of Clark Street and North Avenue, across from the Chicago Historical Society.

Public Transportation: Your best bet is the bus; nos. 11, 22, 36, 151, and 156 all stop at or near the Chicago Historical Society. There are several El stops on the fringes of Old Town; the closest is Sedgwick on the Brown line (about a 15-min. walk away from the start of this tour). On the Red line, the nearest stops are at Clark/Division and North/Clybourn.

Finish: 1211 N. LaSalle Dr. (across from the Clark/Division stop of the Red line train).

Time: 2 hours.

Best Times: Daylight hours and weekends, especially Saturday, when street life is most intense, are best. On stretches along this walk, it's a good idea to exercise reasonable vigilance. Old Town has become increasingly fashionable, but pockets of poverty remain. The relative proximity of Cabrini-Green, one of the most disastrous experiments ever in low-income housing, but now in transition to a mixed-income neighborhood, makes it necessary to issue this word of caution.

Worst Time: After dark (unless the purpose of your visit is to sample Old Town's nightlife).

W hen you consider that Chicago was not officially founded until 1833, the rapid settlement of this area in the 1840s lends historical justification to its designation as "Old Town." The early arrivals were primarily Germans who had begun to flee the Continent in great numbers due to crop failures, famine, and the decline of cottage industry. On this land just north of more "urban" districts (today the Loop, the Near West Side, and River North), the immigrants found the earth suitable for truck farming. They cultivated crops that were staples in their own daily diet: potatoes, cabbage, and celery.

By 1852, German Catholics were plentiful enough to found the parish of St. Michael's, which by the end of the century was the largest German congregation in the city. The farms gradually disappeared as Chicago spread north and Old Town blended into the encroaching urban hustle and bustle. But North Avenue, with its many specialty shops and beer halls, retained its ethnic flavor; for years it was known as "German Broadway." The arrival of substantial industry, like the Oscar Mayer Sausage Company, plus a brewery and a piano factory, provided Old Town with a level of economic self-sufficiency. Many residents were able to duplicate a town life similar to the one they had left behind, living and working in the same community.

The 1871 fire destroyed much of the neighborhood. The walls of St. Michael's withstood the inferno, as did a handful of homes, which are today treasured relics of an early stage of Chicago's life otherwise virtually consumed by the blaze. First shanties, then more permanent wooden cottages, went up in the reconstruction years immediately following the Great Fire. By 1874, rigorous building codes applied to new construction, but much of the interim housing was allowed to stand, and some of it survives to this day. Old Town retained its German flavor well into the 1930s, and even now the many shells of the Germans' clubs and institutions remain as testament to the heyday of that culture.

Gradually the ethnic complexion of Old Town began to change, as a wider spectrum of groups took up residence and the Germans climbed a rung or two on the socioeconomic ladder and moved farther north. By World War II, the neighborhood was in decline, and the stage was set for its discovery by an advance guard of bohemians and artists. The 1960s saw parts of Old Town—especially the Wells Street area—transformed into the Chicago equivalent of Haight-Ashbury or the East Village. In due time, the psychedelic revolution ran its course; the head shops disappeared, but many of the "alternative" theatrical and comedy clubs stayed and prospered. Eventually, the remaining larger businesses—including, in recent years, the Oscar Mayer plant and the Dr. Scholl's factory—closed their doors. With the almost complete gentrification of Lincoln Park to the north and east, Old Town soon became a prime real estate market for people of means who chose to remain near their downtown jobs rather than commute from the suburbs. At present, Old Town combines these two roles: bedroom community for middle- to upper-income Chicagoans and entertainment zone for the entire city, with numerous restaurants and some of the best-known and most respected comedy clubs in the country.

● ● ● ● ● ● ● ● ● ● ● ● ● ● ● ● ●

Our tour begins by taking in a few institutional sites along this stretch of Clark Street. First, at 1536 N. Clark St., is the:

1. **Germania Club.** Among German-Americans, singing societies—known as *Sangvereins*—provided a significant social outlet. The Sangverein originally housed in this elaborately ornamented terra-cotta structure came together in the aftermath of a national tragedy. The club began in 1865 when 300 German-American Civil War veterans formed a men's choir to sing at Abraham Lincoln's funeral. Only with the construction of this hall in 1889 did the Germania Club establish a permanent home. Today, a bank and a few shops occupy a section of the building; you can enter the lobby on the south side.

   Across the street, with its entrance facing North Avenue, is a building of no particular architectural interest but with a notable occupant: it houses the prestigious Latin School of Chicago, founded in 1888. Cross North

Old Town

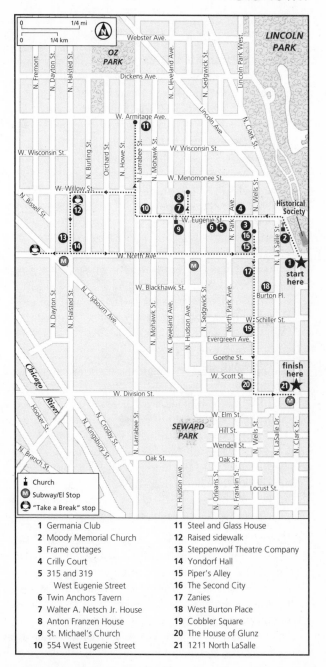

Church
Subway/El Stop
"Take a Break" stop

1 Germania Club	**11** Steel and Glass House
2 Moody Memorial Church	**12** Raised sidewalk
3 Frame cottages	**13** Steppenwolf Theatre Company
4 Crilly Court	**14** Yondorf Hall
5 315 and 319	**15** Piper's Alley
West Eugenie Street	**16** The Second City
6 Twin Anchors Tavern	**17** Zanies
7 Walter A. Netsch Jr. House	**18** West Burton Place
8 Anton Franzen House	**19** Cobbler Square
9 St. Michael's Church	**20** The House of Glunz
10 554 West Eugenie Street	**21** 1211 North LaSalle

Avenue and walk north on the west side of Clark Street.
Directly across from the Chicago Historical Society is the:

2. **Moody Memorial Church.** Dwight L. Moody was one
of a handful of colorful American evangelists who made
his mark internationally by preaching the "old-time religion" of revivalism. Moody came to Chicago from
Massachusetts in 1856 and prospered as a shoe salesman.
He soon turned away from business to undertake missionary work in the city's poorer sections, working initially
under the auspices of the YMCA. Moody's original
church at Chicago Avenue and LaSalle Drive, where the
Moody Bible Institute is now located, rapidly became one
of the largest congregations in the city. The church on
Clark Street was not built until 1925, a quarter-century
after Moody's death. The design incorporates echoes of
the Byzantine and Romanesque, especially the strong
influence of Istanbul's Hagia Sophia.

Walk to the corner by the gas station and cross LaSalle
Drive going west, turning left onto Eugenie Street. Cross
Wells Street and you'll see pre-1874 structures at nos.
215, 217, and 219. These are:

3. **Frame cottages.** The one- and two-story homes went
up between 1871 and 1874, when a tough new city
building ordinance outlawed construction of wooden
houses. Notice how the plainness of the homes' original
trim and design shines through the well-turned contemporary restorations; these were once simple worker's
houses. Also note the unusually high basements, which
rise several feet above street level.

Across the street behind you, occupying an entire
block, is a residential complex known as:

4. **Crilly Court.** Begun by Daniel F. Crilly after 1885,
Crilly Court contained both housing and commercial
space that was geared to people of varying economic
means. Crilly cut a lane, named it for himself, and offered
cottages to working families on the lower end of the economic ladder. These well-maintained row houses and
apartments possess great charm that derives from their
partially sequestered location and their appearance, which
suggests something of an old quarter of New Orleans.

Check out two more vintage cottages up the street:

5. **315 and 319 W. Eugenie St.** These homes are also examples of wooden dwellings built in the years immediately following the Great Fire. They are noteworthy for their slightly more fanciful exterior trim work, by no means rare even in poor immigrant neighborhoods, where so many skilled artisans made their homes.

At the corner of Eugenie and Sedgwick streets is the:

6. **Twin Anchors Tavern.** This neighborhood watering hole was one of the first sports bars in the city. The ribs at the Twin Anchors are also a draw. Among the famous patrons was none other than Old Blue Eyes himself, crooner Frank Sinatra.

Two short blocks west at the corner, 1700 N. Hudson Ave., is the home of a contemporary architect generally known for his work on a larger scale, the:

7. **Walter A. Netsch Jr. House.** Netsch was once a partner at the architectural mega-firm of Skidmore, Owings & Merrill. He designed the Air Force Academy Chapel and the rather bleak, ultramodern University of Illinois at Chicago campus, which occupies the land just west of the Loop where many Hull House Settlement buildings once stood. For his own home (1974), he followed a tradition favored in Europe during the Middle Ages, in which domestic space is oriented inward, away from the street. Stand near the garage and look up through the back window for a glimpse of the central loft, which rises 33 feet. By day, it gets light and heat from skylights equipped with passive solar panels.

A brief detour to 1726 N. Hudson Ave. reveals an interesting example of the cottages built just after the 1874 building ordinance, the:

8. **Anton Franzen House.** If there is such a thing as a representative Chicago house, this cottage is the classic type. Frank Lloyd Wright's original Oak Park cottage was not so different in appearance from this demure story-and-a-half with its broad gabled facade. The distinguishing feature of the Franzen House, built in 1880, is its brick—rather than wood—construction.

Next make your way back to Eugenie. On the square at the end of the street is the monumental:

9. **St. Michael's Church.** In the first half of the 19th century, the two major branches of the Roman Catholic Church in America were the Irish and the German. The German national parishes attained a fair degree of autonomy in preserving their unique liturgical practices and in the observance of culturally determined feast days. The feast of Corpus Christi, for example, inspired a level of pageantry among German Catholics that was unknown among the Irish. Looking at St. Michael's, one can easily conjure up an image of ceremonial grandeur to match the scale of the fine, massive Romanesque temple.

Inside, the southern European influence on the elaborate baroque appointments is apparent. The stained glass windows were imported from Munich at the beginning of the 20th century. As if guarding the vaults that lead to heaven, an effigy of the archangel Michael hovers over the faithful. In the Catholic iconography, St. Michael, who drove the proud and disobedient Adam and Eve from Paradise, occupies a powerful position. This final plea at the end of every mass during the days of the old Tridentine liturgy ("St. Michael the Archangel, defend us in battle against the wickedness and snares of the devil . . .") was one of the few spoken in English before the sweeping reforms of Vatican II replaced Latin with the vernacular. The church's clock tower still presides over the neighborhood like a beacon. It's said that you're in Old Town when you're within earshot of St. Michael's bells.

Crossing the great apron that spans the courtyard before the entrance to St. Michael's, we again pick up Eugenie Street and move on to one of the more unusual homes in the neighborhood:

10. **554 W. Eugenie St.** As you stand before this oddly appealing edifice, it is not immediately obvious exactly what you are looking at. Is it a futuristic house of worship? A snappy commercial building? A nest of avantgarde apartments? Two semidetached homes? Suspended between two apparently separate structures is a belfry,

housing a molded object whose geometric shape must certainly owe something to the influence of the Prairie School. Nor is that the only reverberation of past architectural styles patched throughout the exterior of this 1991 postmodern fantasy, which, somewhat anticlimactically, turns out to be a single-family dwelling. The tower, incidentally, pays homage to its counterpart at neighboring St. Michael's.

Turn north (right) on Larrabee Street and walk along three long blocks of rather bland, insular town houses. An unusual dwelling at the end of this block at no. 1949, near Armitage, is known as the:

11. **Steel and Glass House.** Built in 1949 (and thoroughly revamped 30 years later), this home represents the post–World War II architecture of optimism at its most daring. The steel-framed house, wrapped in glass around 5,000 square feet of interior space, looks at first suspiciously like one of those modified-Miesian grade schools that popped up everywhere in the United States in the 1950s. Much of the beguiling interior, however, is visible from the outside—such is the price paid by those who live in glass houses—and this softens considerably the initial impression of something cold and institutional.

Double back to Willow Street and continue west until you reach Halsted. As you will have noticed by now, this section of Old Town is an architectural showcase. Many princely homes sit among the troll-like pillbox row houses and suburban-style garden apartments that make you keep looking over your shoulder for signs of the nearest shopping mall. Well, we can't deliver the mall, but a bona fide entertainment and nightlife strip, dotted with many tiny boutiques, looms on the horizon. The Halsted strip, with its host of power shops and restaurants (Abercrombie & Fitch, the Gap, and Café Ba-Ba-Reeba!, to drop just a few of the more recognizable names) trails off beyond Old Town to the north, running from Willow Street to Fullerton and beyond. File this away for future reference, because our path takes us in the opposite direction.

Take a Break Drop into **Pizza Capri,** 1733 N. Halsted St., near Willow, one block above North Avenue (☎ **312/280-5700**). Try a slice of a specialty pizza, like Thai pie or veggie twist, or select from a menu that includes pasta dishes, salads, and milk and cookies.

As we walk south (left) down Halsted toward North Avenue, there are several landmarks along the way. First is the:

12. **Raised sidewalk in front of 1713 N. Halsted.** This is a rare relic of the generally seamless transformation of the urban landscape from one epoch to the next. The roadway was raised, and the old house remained down in the hollow.

Next, at 1650 N. Halsted, is the city's reigning off-Loop theater:

13. **Steppenwolf Theatre Company.** Steppenwolf began as a shoestring operation nurtured by the artistic capital of its associated actors (John Malkovich, Gary Sinise, Joan Allen, and Laurie Metcalf, among other luminaries), directors, and supporters. In recent years it has become one of the few regional theaters that can lay claim to national prominence. If you pass by around show time, inquire about half-price rush tickets, which go on sale one hour before each performance.

While you're walking along Halsted, you also may notice the street's striped bicycle lanes, a growing effort to make the city more accessible to two-wheel commuters.

On the corner of Halsted at 758 W. North Ave. is a large building housing a bank. This is the former:

14. **Yondorf Hall.** The German-American community in general was so club-minded, and the demand for meeting space so great, that private halls provided entrepreneurial builders with viable investment opportunities. It was not unusual for active German-American men to hold membership simultaneously in three or four lodges, singing clubs, or political or religious fraternal societies. They attended weekly meetings decked out in the regalia of each organization. The Yondorf Building, built in 1887, contained six separate halls. The principal one, a vast space on the third floor equipped with a stage and gallery,

remains empty today. Though partially renovated, it retains much of its period character and charm. The hall is not open to the public; some of the building now houses administrative offices for Steppenwolf.

The corner of Halsted and North Avenue is a vantage point for several points of interest. A block to your west, Clybourn Avenue crosses North Avenue. This is the beginning of the so-called Clybourn Corridor, a district filled with old red-brick manufactories formerly employed by light industry. The area has rapidly transformed into a mixed residential and entertainment zone that includes shopping centers (anchored by the largest Crate & Barrel in the city), restaurants, and nightclubs.

Take a Break It's a bit of a stretch, and a detour from our route, but the **Goose Island Brewing Co.,** 1800 N. Clybourn Ave. (☎ **312/915-0073**), is worth the effort. The only drawback is that once you've discovered the Goose Island Brewery, you may never get back to the tour. The two main draws are the food—like veggie chili, fish and chips, and many delicious appetizers and sandwiches—and the beer, brewed on the premises in 40 spectacular varieties, only a half dozen of which are available in any given season. Order a beer sampler to taste a few at a time.

Our tour continues at Wells Street, Old Town's main drag, approximately half a mile to the east. To get there from Halsted, you have three options. You can hail a cab if you're so inclined (and lucky); you can hop the North Avenue bus; or you can walk. At a brisk pace you can cover the ground quickly, as there's nothing much to see.

On the northwest corner of North Avenue, at 1608 N. Wells St., is:

15. **Piper's Alley.** This entertainment space was the site of a bakery owned by Henry Piper in 1880. It was Old Town's most popular tourist attraction during the 1960s, when it was filled with boutiques and head shops. Today it is still home to an art-film cinema (one of the venues for the annual Chicago International Film Festival), a couple of theaters, and, at the entrance at 1616 N. Wells St., the esteemed comedy club:

16. **The Second City.** Since the mid-1950s, the hothouse humor of Chicago has become the mainstream humor of the nation. It began with Mike Nichols and Elaine May. They gained their spurs in Chicago at clubs like this one, and then won a national audience on early television with biting psycho-satires that incorporated the traditional skit-based humor of vaudeville. This was Lenny Bruce with dentures. Nichols and May plated their sarcasm with cynical smiles; they were seldom vulgar and never overtly subversive. Many great stars have followed the tightrope path those two blazed. Among the spiritual protégés who've played this club are Robert Klein, John Belushi, Joan Rivers, Bill Murray, Shelley Long, Robin Williams, and Mike Myers. Who's next? You'll have to go to find out.

    In the same pattern is another club down the block, just south of North Avenue at 1548 N. Wells St.:

17. **Zanies.** The routines at this comedy club, which opened in 1978, are well polished. The headliners have proven themselves before national audiences on "The Tonight Show," David Letterman, HBO, Showtime, and so forth.

    An unusual constellation of homes is our next point of interest on:

18. **West Burton Place.** Enter this short block (formerly called Carl St.) from the Wells Street side, by way of the Burton Place plaza. Many of these buildings, originally standard cookie-cutter Victorian homes, have been remodeled beyond recognition into apartment buildings. The remodeling, moreover, had the force of an artistic statement. A collaborative effort, it was the inspiration of two men, Sol Kagen and Edgar Miller, who had studied together in 1917 at the School of the Art Institute. The gist of their visions could be summed up as handyman rehabs with salvaged and found materials. Today, leases on apartments like those in 155 W. Burton Place, considered Miller's masterpiece, are preciously guarded. As for 151 W. Burton Place, try to unravel the steps it took to alter the old Victorian outline of this house into the charming Art Deco form of its contemporary exterior.

Another interesting example of Edgar Miller's work lies one block south at 154 W. Schiller St.

Between Schiller and Evergreen at 1350 N. Wells St. is another development with interesting historical roots, mixing residential and commercial uses:

19. **Cobbler Square.** Roughly 20 existing buildings went into this postmodern confection. The oldest piece of the pie, dating from 1880, was the assembly plant of a bicycle manufacturer called Western Wheel Works. The legendary William M. Scholl bought the factory in 1911. Yes, Virginia, there was a real Dr. Scholl, and he founded his foot-care accessory business right here on Wells Street. Some of today's retail tenants include a branch of Barbara's Bookstore and Pier 1 Imports. Most of the other tenants occupy some 295 residential units.

There's an odd duck of a retail store close to Division Street at 1206 N. Wells St.:

20. **The House of Glunz.** This famous Old Town wine emporium dates from 1888, when a farmer from Westphalia decided to settle in the city and change his profession. During Prohibition, Glunz managed to stay afloat by selling altar wine and products used for manufacturing wine at home. Today, The House of Glunz is one of the most respected wine merchants in Chicago, with a cellar storing some 1,300 wines. Wine-tasting events usually take place on Saturday; there's an annual tasting of rare and fine Madeiras in November. If the store is open and the owner willing, take a look at the collection of old bottles, crystal, and cooper's tools in the museum room. The owner recently restored the facade of the building, which dates to 1 year before the Chicago Fire, to its original 19th-century appearance.

Our final stop takes us two blocks east along Division Street to:

21. **1211 N. LaSalle.** Mural artist Richard Haas's *trompe l'oeil* paintings on the facades of public and private buildings, here and in Europe, have encouraged a welcome trend to liven up the urban landscape. You can hardly go to an American city and not see a detailed, hyper-realist

representation of windows, or a cartoon facade of a text-book classical temple, painted on what was formerly the blank wall of a boring downtown building. This sample of Haas's handiwork, covering the walls of a converted apartment building from head to foot, is a crown jewel of the genre. He calls this work *Homage to the Chicago School of Architecture.* The eye-catching centerpiece, facing Division Street, is the reproduction of Sullivan's *Golden Doorway* from the Transportation Building of the 1893 World's Columbian Exposition.

Lincoln Park

Start: The grounds of the Chicago Historical Society, Clark Street at North Avenue, at the southern end of Lincoln Park.

Public Transportation: CTA bus nos. 11, 22, 36, 72, 151, and 156 stop nearby. The closest El stop is Sedgwick on the Brown line (about a 15-min. walk away from the start of this tour). On the Red line, the nearest stops are at Clark/Division and North/Clybourn.

Finish: The Chicago Historical Society.

Time: 1½ hours for the walk; add 2 hours if you decide to really explore the zoo and the two museums on this itinerary.

Best Times: Try to go when the zoo and museums are open. Museum schedules appear below; the zoo grounds are open daily from 8am to 5pm (buildings 9am–5pm) with later weekend and summer hours.

Worst Times: When the zoo and museums are closed.

Lincoln Park is the largest and most popular park in Chicago. Long and narrow, the park follows Lake Michigan's shoreline for almost 6 miles and encompasses more than 1,200 acres. In the summertime, Lincoln Park virtually spills over with crowds who gather to take their leisure in a variety of ways, especially on the weekends, and most heavily at the lakefront beaches. The park and one of its principal attractions, the zoo, are open year-round, so a visit is never really out of season.

This walking tour concentrates on four main elements: the park, the zoo, a stroll down Lincoln Park West, and a visit to a museum, the Chicago Historical Society. Our walk through the park will focus primarily on a detailed exploration of the attractive Lincoln Park Zoo, the oldest zoo in the country and one of the last free ones. The zoo makes for a sylvan stroll in the city. But for some visitors, the rather compact nature of the exhibits (despite major overhauls in recent years) may leave them feeling rather sad to encounter these wild creatures in an urban setting. The tour will highlight a handful of other park attractions that fall within the area we'll be visiting, between North and Belden avenues.

● ● ● ● ● ● ● ● ● ● ● ● ● ● ● ●

Our tour begins on the grounds east of the Historical Society, at the:

1. **Statue of Abraham Lincoln.** This impressive monument, also known as The Standing Lincoln, was completed in 1887 by the Dublin-born sculptor Augustus Saint-Gaudens. (His Seated Lincoln is at Grant Park.) Saint-Gaudens, the son of an Irish mother and French father, was brought to New York City as an infant and apprenticed at age 13 to a cameo cutter. He became the most celebrated American sculptor of the late 19th century. The subject of Lincoln was dear to Saint-Gaudens, who executed two major likenesses of the fallen president. He based his designs to some degree on personal observations, once when the president was alive, and then again when Lincoln's remains laid in state. This work, which shows the president poised to begin a public address, also benefits from the life casts of Lincoln's face and hands executed by the sculptor Leonard Volk.

   Now, follow the path north and enter the park by way of a subterranean walk under LaSalle. Continue on the formal, tree-lined path, passing a statue of Benjamin Franklin, and along the South Pond to the entrance of the:

Lincoln Park

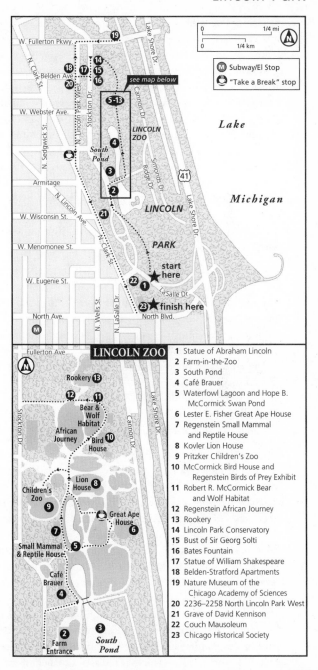

LINCOLN ZOO

Rookery 13

12

11

Bear & Wolf Habitat

African Journey

Bird House 10

Children's Zoo

Lion House 8

9

Great Ape House

7

Small Mammal & Reptile House

5

Café Brauer

4

2 Farm Entrance

3 South Pond

Subway/El Stop

"Take a Break" stop

1 Statue of Abraham Lincoln
2 Farm-in-the-Zoo
3 South Pond
4 Café Brauer
5 Waterfowl Lagoon and Hope B. McCormick Swan Pond
6 Lester E. Fisher Great Ape House
7 Regenstein Small Mammal and Reptile House
8 Kovler Lion House
9 Pritzker Children's Zoo
10 McCormick Bird House and Regenstein Birds of Prey Exhibit
11 Robert R. McCormick Bear and Wolf Habitat
12 Regenstein African Journey
13 Rookery
14 Lincoln Park Conservatory
15 Bust of Sir Georg Solti
16 Bates Fountain
17 Statue of William Shakespeare
18 Belden-Stratford Apartments
19 Nature Museum of the Chicago Academy of Sciences
20 2236–2258 North Lincoln Park West
21 Grave of David Kennison
22 Couch Mausoleum
23 Chicago Historical Society

2. **Farm-in-the-Zoo.** This replica of a farm on the prairie was completed in the 1960s and was recently completely renovated and updated. Featured on the 5-acre plot are a working dairy barn, a livestock shed, a poultry coop, and a beehive. The barnlike educational facility schedules programs that help urban residents understand the importance of agriculture and the American farmer (and there are plenty of interactive exhibits to appeal to computer-savvy kids). This is very much a hands-on facility and is particularly popular with school-age children. The Farm-in-the-Zoo's cows yield about 20 gallons of fresh milk daily, and the 30 or so chickens lay an average of 2 dozen eggs a week.

When you exit the farm, continue on the path along the:

3. **South Pond.** South Pond is a perennial favorite among Chicagoans for paddle boating. In winters past, it provided an outdoor pond for ice-skating as well. Here the zoo had its modest beginnings in 1868, when the park received a pair of trumpeter swans as a gift from the Central Park Zoo in New York City. The swan, whose image appears throughout the park, remains the symbol of the Lincoln Park Zoo.

The splendid building ahead to your immediate left as you walk across a small bridge is a landmark, listed on the National Register of Historic Places:

4. **Café Brauer.** This stunning Prairie-style cafe was built in 1908 to replace a large Victorian boathouse that once occupied this spot on the edge of the lagoon. The cafe, which operated as a Continental-style restaurant between 1912 and 1941, now houses a cafeteria, an ice cream shop, and a lovely second-floor banquet hall that's available for private parties (it's not open to the public, but you may be able to sneak a peek if the staff is setting up for a special event). Outside Café Brauer you can also rent paddle boats.

Just beyond Café Brauer is an entrance to the zoo. Our tour will be abbreviated, highlighting some of the 35•acre zoo's most popular attractions. You may want to head directly to the east gate where the Gateway Pavilion welcomes visitors with an information desk and a variety of services that include: lockers, first aid, lost and found, stroller rental, and free wheelchairs. If you remain at the zoo's south gate, walk around to the right to view our first stop, the:

5. **Waterfowl Lagoon and Hope B. McCormick Swan Pond.** The zoo honored its beginnings with an attractive renovation of the swan pond, now home to a new pair of snowy-white trumpeter swans. On the other side of a footbridge is a new Waterfowl Lagoon, where a flock of Caribbean pink flamingos wade (certainly a surreal image in Chicago), and more than 20 species of migrating birds make pit stops among the native Illinois plants and wild-flowers. From here, reverse your direction and follow the signs toward the:

6. **Regenstein Center for African Apes.** The zoo's orig-inal Great Ape House opened in 1976 to show off one of the most successful lowland gorilla collections in the United States. More than 40 gorillas have been born in the zoo. The building is currently undergoing a complete renovation, however, and the zoo's gorillas and chimps have been moved temporarily to other zoos. Look for the new, improved Ape House to open in 2004.

As you leave the Ape House, you'll see the Primate House on your right, then the old Reptile House, built in 1923 as the city's first aquarium. It reopened in 1998 as Park Pavilion, a year-round food court with indoor and terrace seating. Across the swan pond is one of the zoo's most ambitious new projects, the:

7. **Regenstein Small Mammal-Reptile House.** Replacing the old reptile quarters, this modern $12 mil-lion facility, which opened in 1997, is easily one of the highlights of a visit. The 32,000-square-foot building combines two fascinating exhibits. The first is a gallery area that puts visitors eye-to-eye with warm- and cold-blooded creatures. You peer through large windows into the habitats of boas and naked mole rats, and, in an appropriately dark nook, a bat cave. All the barriers fall when visitors move under the 45-foot glass dome of the adjoining Ecosystem, where you walk through habitats of four continents, including tropical rain forest, savanna,

Bushman & Perkins: National Celebrities at the Lincoln Park Zoo

On August 15, 1930, a 38-pound, 2½-year-old gorilla from French Cameroon arrived at the Lincoln Park Zoo. At the time, he was one of only five gorillas in captivity. At full maturity, Bushman weighed in at 550 pounds. By the time he died in 1951, Bushman had achieved a celebrity status way beyond the confines of Chicago. Notre Dame coach Knute Rockne, hearing that Bushman liked to play football, sent the gorilla an autographed ball. Members of the Alexander Dumas Gourmand Club in France made Bushman an honorary member when they learned that he had devoured 22 pounds of food at one sitting. Bushman appeared countless times in newsreels and on the pages of such national magazines as *Look* and *Life*. When Bushman died, thousands filed past his empty cage to pay their last respects, and the interior of the Monkey House was renamed Bushman Hall in his honor.

Marlin Perkins was a primate, too, though most of the time he lived outside the cages where the other zoo residents reside. Perkins was a director of the zoo who rose to national prominence on *Zoo Parade,* an NBC-TV nature show that ran from 1949 to 1957 and was broadcasted weekly from the Lincoln Park Zoo. Perkins then moved on to the equally popular *Wild Kingdom,* which also aired for many years. Perkins's public leadership role is credited with having made Lincoln Park Zoo the most visited zoo in the world during the 1950s— as it is today—with an annual attendance exceeding 3 million.

and desert. The 200 eminently intriguing animals who live here—cotton-top tamarins, African dwarf crocodiles, and countless exotic birds—aren't segregated by species but mixed in settings that give you a feel for the worlds they inhabit.

Now walk toward the central plaza of the zoo and the:

8. **Kovler Lion House.** This combination den enclosure and naturalistic outdoor habitat is home to the zoo's world-class collection of endangered and threatened big cats. Tiger aficionados will especially like this exhibit: There are huge slinky Siberians, and the Bengals can be seen lounging about in their newly refurbished front yard, separated from their potential human prey by a wide, deep moat. Some of the other beautiful cats are snow leopards, cheetahs, and pumas.

   On the way to our next stop, you'll no doubt be charmed by the energetic residents of the Sea Lion Pool, a 225,000-gallon tank patrolled by several harbor seals and California sea lions. Feeding time is always a popular attraction. Around the pool near one of the zoo entrances is another kid-pleaser, the:

9. **Pritzker Children's Zoo.** When it opened in 1959, this was the first indoor children's zoo in the country. The central attraction is a display of North American wildlife in an exotic garden setting. During warm weather, educational live-animal presentations take place in the outdoor amphitheater. The zoo's nursery is also here, as is a petting zoo where the kids can inspect an array of creatures: maybe a salamander, an owl, or a hedgehog. Another popular educational program, "Conservation Station," is a hands-on learning center for children.

   Now cross over to the eastern side of the zoo and follow the signs to the:

10. **McCormick Bird House and Regenstein Birds of Prey Exhibit.** Originally opened in 1904, the Bird House recently reopened after a $2.8 million renovation. The overhauled building contains 10 new and improved habitats re-creating six different ecosystems with lush landscaping. Take your chances in the free-flight area; once an exotic bird landed on my shoulder, which I took as a good omen. (Of course, there's always the possibility that something else might land on your shoulder.)

There's a catch-22 provision associated with the Birds of Prey Exhibit: Some species can't be kept in captivity unless there's something wrong with them. The bald eagles on display, for example, are among the walking wounded; one is lame, the other blind. Also in residence here are the usual gang of road-kill scavengers, owls, vultures, and a host of other well-loved raptors.

Nearby is the:

11. **Robert R. McCormick Bear and Wolf Habitat.** The main attraction here is a 266,000-gallon polar bear pool with an underwater viewing window. The wolf, too, is an endless source of fascination.

Near the Bear and Wolf Habitat, construction is under way on the:

12. **Regenstein African Journey.** This extensive new exhibition provides a new, enhanced environment for the zoo's large mammals, who previously spent much of their time stuck in either indoor cages or a limited outdoor area. Scheduled to open this year, the Regenstein African Journey creates more natural habitats for giraffes, rhinos, elephants, wild dogs, ostriches, and other African animals.

Our tour of the zoo ends here. Exit by way of the Conservatory entrance. Before leaving, check to see if one special environment is open to the public. Weather permitting, you may see the:

13. **Rookery.** Alfred Caldwell redesigned this former Victorian lily pond in 1937. Both Japanese formalism and the Prairie style inspired its plantings and stonework. The pond had become overgrown and woodsy in recent years, but a recent renovation cleared out the weeds and broken stones, and now the area is a pleasant spot to sit and contemplate. Birdwatchers may find some interesting species passing through here; the Rookery is a popular spot for migrating birds.

On the way out of the park there are several other points of interest, including the:

14. **Lincoln Park Conservatory.** Inside are four great halls, built between 1890 and 1895, filled with thousands of plants. This is the closest thing Chicago has to a botanical garden within the city limits. The Palm House is

resplendent with giant palms and rubber trees, the Fernery nurtures plants that grow close to the forest floor, and the Tropical House is a symphony of shiny greenery. The fourth hall, Show House, focuses on seasonal floral exhibitions. The conservatory is open daily from 9am to 5pm; admission is free.

A few paces south of the conservatory entrance is a large, modern sculpture, the:

15. **Bust of Sir Georg Solti.** Until his retirement in the early 1990s, Solti was so highly regarded as the musical director of the Chicago Symphony that he rated a public statue while still living. It now serves as an enduring tribute to Solti, who died in 1997.

Beyond the homage to Solti is a French formal garden, a magnificent sight to behold from late spring to October. The thoughtfully placed benches are fine spots to spend an afternoon reading or enjoying the day. In the midst of the garden is the:

16. **Bates Fountain.** Also known as "Storks at Play," the fountain is the combined work of Augustus Saint-Gaudens and his former student, Frederick William MacMonnies.

Leave the park along the path that runs in front of the conservatory; on your way to the street, you'll pass through an English garden, selectively planted with a variety of trees and shrubs and many lovely flowers. Just before emerging onto Lincoln Park West at Belden Avenue, behold the statue of the seated:

17. **William Shakespeare.** This is one of many public statues in the park whose upkeep has corporate sponsorship thanks to the "Adopt a Monument" program promoted by a group called Friends of Lincoln Park. Among the other statues under the group's care are those of LaSalle, Schiller, Franklin, Grant, Goethe, and Hans Christian Andersen.

Across the street is an apartment building, 2300 N. Lincoln Park W., that once functioned as a swank North Side hotel, the:

18. **Belden-Stratford Apartments.** For culinary sophisticates, the most interesting thing about this building is that it is home to two fine restaurants, the French bistro

Mon Ami Gabi and the super-chic Ambria, one of the best French restaurants in the city. Whether or not you eat at these worthy establishments, take a moment now to enter the Belden-Stratford and see the lobby. If possible, peek inside the Ambria dining room, a paradigm of Continental elegance.

From here you may consider taking a short detour north to Fullerton Parkway and Cannon Drive to visit the new home of another Lincoln Park institution, the:

19. **Peggy Notebaert Nature Museum of the Chicago Academy of Sciences.** Beginning in 1893, the Academy housed its natural history collection in what is now the Lincoln Park Zoo administration building. A new state-of-the-art facility (☎ 773/755-5100; www.chias.org) for Chicago's oldest museum (dating to 1857) opened on the edge of the park's North Pond in 1999. A variety of permanent exhibitions examine the relationship between people and nature, with emphasis on the natural world of Chicago and the Midwest. Many of the exhibits are geared toward kids, making this a good stop for families. A highlight is a butterfly greenhouse that is home to more than 500 butterflies and moths. A thicket of native plants and wildflowers grows on the grounds of the building.

Now take a leisurely stroll south along Lincoln Park West. There are two sites to point out along this route, less for their intrinsic value than for their link to Chicago's two most revered architects:

20. **2236–2258 N. Lincoln Park W.** Simeon B. Eisendrath, an apprentice in the firm of Louis H. Sullivan, designed this block of apartments. Farther down the avenue, you'll see 2103–2117 N. Clark St. and 310–312 W. Dickens Ave.; the architect Frank Lloyd Wright first worked for when he arrived in Chicago, Joseph Lyman Silsbee (who also worked on the Lincoln Park Conservatory), designed these row houses.

Take a Break Also on the corner at Dickens Avenue is **R. J. Grunts,** 2056 Lincoln Park West (☎ 773/929-5363). This popular neighborhood restaurant offers an extensive menu of chicken dishes, burgers,

Robert Kennicott, Founder of the Academy of Sciences

This obscure naturalist, who died in 1866 at the age of 31 during an expedition in the Yukon, was one of the most promising young scientists of his day. He was only 22 when he helped to found the Academy of Sciences, which was based substantially on specimens Kennicott had collected during his youth and while conducting a survey of natural resources on land belonging to the Illinois Central Railroad. Kennicott's explorations made him one of the first white men to visit regions of the Arctic in Alaska and Canada. At the time of his death, he had not only assembled what is often referred to as the most extensive collection of plant and animal speci- mens of the 19th century, but he had also compiled eyewitness reports from Alaska that reportedly helped convince the U.S. government to purchase the territory from Russia. While on an expedition in 1866 to help survey a telegraph route to Europe across the Bering Strait and Siberia, Kennicott rescued a Russian whose boat had begun to sink from the freezing water. The man had stolen the boat and was attempting to abandon the expedition. The next morning, Kennicott's body was found on a beach of the Yukon River—his death the apparent result of a heart attack. Before dying, he had scratched a map of the surrounding region in the sand.

pasta plates, and the like. There's also a first-rate salad bar (when the restaurant opened in the 1970s, this was the 1st salad bar in the city—quite a novelty at the time). The knockout all-you-can-eat Sunday brunch is sometimes too crowded to accommodate all comers. The commem- orative brown street sign announces that this block has been given the honorific name "Richard Melman Place." It recognizes the city's hometown restaurant mogul, who launched his Lettuce Entertain You empire more than two decades ago with this neighborhood spot.

Follow Lincoln Park West south until it intersects with Clark Street, and then head south on Clark. A strip of parkland runs along Clark Street near the Farm-in-the-Zoo. Here, across from the intersection of Clark and Wisconsin streets, you will find a most unusual sight on a large boulder marked with a plaque, the:

21. **Grave of David Kennison.** Most of what is today the southern end of Lincoln Park was once Chicago's municipal cemetery, running from North to Webster avenues. Re-interment of the many remains within burial grounds outside the city limits was not completed until 1874, almost a decade after the park opened. Somehow, the grave of this historic figure remained undisturbed. Kennison was truly one of a kind. He was born in 1736 and died 115 years later, in 1852. His lifetime spanned the French and Indian War, the Revolutionary War, and the Boston Tea Party, of which, according to legend, he was the oldest surviving participant.

Continue on Clark Street to our final stop. After crossing LaSalle, you will pass, on your left (just west of the gas station), the:

22. **Couch Mausoleum.** Surrounded by a wrought-iron fence, this unusual site is the only family tomb that remains from the old cemetery. The Couch family went all the way to the Illinois Supreme Court in an effort to block its removal. In a final macabre note about the old municipal cemetery, now and then when the city digs here for one purpose or another, a few spare bones turn up.

We have now come full circle, and our final treat is a visit to one of the city's most interesting museums, the:

23. **Chicago Historical Society,** Clark Street at North Avenue (☎ 312/642-4600; www.chicagohs.org). "People make history. But it's the objects they leave behind . . . that allow us to interpret the past." That line from the Historical Society brochure sums up with elegant simplicity the enduring appeal of this institution's collection. Those objects, as displayed in the Chicago Historical Society, especially in the American Wing, are as compelling

and evocative as any I have ever seen. History buffs will find it hard to tear themselves away from two exhibits in particular, "We the People" (about how "ordinary people" founded the United States of America) and "A House Divided: America in the Age of Lincoln." The gift shop is also worthy of mention for its many books treating various themes of Chicago's past.

The collection merits an extended visit, but for those whose time is limited, or who have simply run out of gas absorbing the other sights along the way, the following abbreviated list of "not to be missed items" can be viewed in just a half hour:

- Benjamin West's 1771 painting, *Penn's Treaty with the Indians*
- Paul Revere's engraving of the 1770 Boston Massacre
- One of 23 surviving copies of the broadside of the Declaration of Independence, printed in Philadelphia on the evening of July 4, 1776
- A powder horn engraved by a Revolutionary War soldier with such symbols as the Tree of Liberty
- An original watercolor sketch of the first rendering of the U.S. flag authorized by the Continental Congress in 1777
- The U.S. Constitution as first printed in a Philadelphia newspaper, along with an original version of the Bill of Rights with 17 amendments
- *The Railsplitter,* an unknown artist's painting of Lincoln displayed at Republican Party rallies during the 1860 election
- Slave shackles and slave tags
- A first printing of *Uncle Tom's Cabin*
- John Brown's Bible
- The table on which Lincoln drafted the Emancipation Proclamation, and a commemorative copy of the 13th Amendment abolishing slavery, signed by Lincoln, among other government officials
- Lincoln's last dispatch to Grant, and the table on which Lee signed the surrender at Appomattox
- Lincoln's deathbed, and Alonzo Chappel's 1868 painting, *The Death of Lincoln*

Winding Down **The Big Shoulders Café,** in a corner wing of the Chicago Historical Society, offers one of the most interesting light menus in the city. The London broil salad is delicious, as is the jalapeño cornbread served with each meal.

The Chicago Historical Society is open Monday to Saturday from 9:30am to 4:30pm, Sunday from 11am to 5pm. Admission is $5 for adults; $1 for children 6 to 12; the museum is free on Mondays.

Wicker Park

Start: Six-corner intersection of Milwaukee, North and Damen avenues.

Public Transportation: Take the Blue line (O'Hare) train to the Damen Avenue stop.

Finish: Caffe de Luca, 1721 N. Damen Ave.

Time: 2 to 3 hours.

Best Time: Any time during the day.

Worst Time: Night.

Wicker Park, a mere 15-minute El ride from downtown on North Milwaukee Avenue, began as an immigrant neighborhood around 1870. Middle-class artisans, mostly Germans and Scandinavians, settled here, as did a few dozen wealthy families. Their fortunes could justify luxurious homes and lifestyles, but their foreign roots made them unwelcome or uncomfortable among their Anglo-American counterparts who were then taking up residence along the Gold Coast.

During the neighborhood's heyday, a 20-year span between 1870 and 1890, the foreign born constituted 44% of Chicago's population; among residents of Wicker Park, the immigrant element during those years climbed from 63% to an astonishing 96%.

The homes these successful entrepreneurs built near Wicker Park, many of which have been preserved, were renowned for their grace and eclectic styling. The neighborhood has undergone many transformations, from lace-curtain respectability to rooming house shabbiness to immigrant way station of the working poor. Today Wicker Park is home to a multiracial community and one of the country's richest settlements of artists; a gradual process of gentrification has restored some of its landmark houses to their former stateliness. Large parts of the neighborhood, including the commercial buildings along Milwaukee Avenue, appear much the way they did at the turn of the century. What's new are the town houses and converted lofts so coveted by urban dwellers, who have been drawn to what was once a relatively inexpensive alternative for people priced out of Lincoln Park and other desirable North Side neighborhoods.

The names of many notable families and personalities are historically associated with Wicker Park. Two of the city's great family fortunes, those of the Pritzkers and the Crowns, originated here. (Arie Crown, a Lithuanian Jew, once sold suspenders along Milwaukee Ave.) Carl Laemmle, founder of Universal Studios, and Mike Todd, the Hollywood director, both lived here, as did authors Nelson Algren, Saul Bellow, and Studs Terkel. Wicker Park has been designated a historic landmark area and has been placed on the National Register of Historic Places.

● ● ● ● ● ● ● ● ● ● ● ● ● ● ● ● ●

To begin our tour, walk south from North Avenue 1 block along Damen Avenue to the edge of:

1. **Wicker Park,** the smallest park in Chicago. Two brothers who were beginning to develop their extensive real estate holdings in the area donated the land to the city around 1870. By setting aside this 4-acre plot as a green space or common, Charles Wicker, an alderman from the 3rd Ward who made his money building railroads, and his brother Joel, a lawyer and bank director, hoped to make their development more attractive to potential builders and investors. Apparently their strategy succeeded. Little

Wicker Park

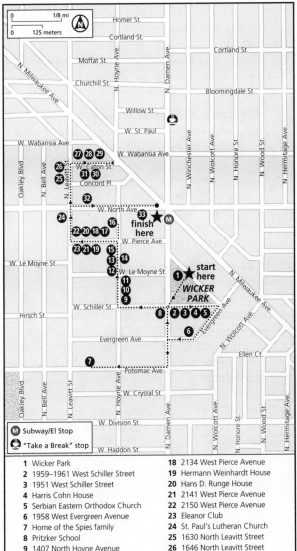

1 Wicker Park
2 1959–1961 West Schiller Street
3 1951 West Schiller Street
4 Harris Cohn House
5 Serbian Eastern Orthodox Church
6 1958 West Evergreen Avenue
7 Home of the Spies family
8 Pritzker School
9 1407 North Hoyne Avenue
10 1417 North Hoyne Avenue
11 1427 North Hoyne Avenue
12 Wicker Park Lutheran Church
13 1520 North Hoyne Avenue
14 1521 North Hoyne Avenue
15 1530 North Hoyne Avenue
16 1558 North Hoyne Avenue
17 2118 West Pierce Avenue
18 2134 West Pierce Avenue
19 Hermann Weinhardt House
20 Hans D. Runge House
21 2141 West Pierce Avenue
22 2150 West Pierce Avenue
23 Eleanor Club
24 St. Paul's Lutheran Church
25 1630 North Leavitt Street
26 1646 North Leavitt Street
27 2156 West Caton Street
28 2152 West Caton Street
29 2142 West Caton Street
30 2145 West Caton Street
31 2147 West Caton Street
32 Association House of Chicago
33 Luxor Baths

remains of the park's 19th-century landscaping, which once included a large manmade pond spanned by a rustic bridge.

Cross the park to the corner of Damen Avenue and Schiller Street. We will follow Schiller the length of the park, walking east. The first stop is:

2. **1959–1961 W. Schiller St.** Built in 1886 for a ship's captain and a medical doctor, this double home reflects the fashionable Second Empire style. The building became a rooming house in the 1920s, but it has been restored in recent years. Note the lively Victorian colors of the cornices, tower, and trim. Other distinctive features are the large mansard roof and the decorative sawtooth pattern in the brickwork.

Next we move to:

3. **1951 W. Schiller St.** When Dr. Nels T. Quales, a native of Norway, had this house built in 1873, he opted for Italianate styling with a Romanesque Revival facade, most notable for its use of arches and truncated columns. Originally, the house was set back much farther from the street. The addition of Moorish windows on the first and second stories altered the facade around 1890; extensive restoration of the house is currently under way. Dr. Quales was a humanitarian who founded Chicago's Lutheran Deaconess Hospital; for this and his many other good works, the King of Norway awarded him the Order of St. Olaf in 1910.

At 1941 W. Schiller St., pause before the:

4. **Harris Cohn House,** also known as the Wicker Park Castle. Mr. Cohn was a clothing manufacturer who commissioned this piece of domestic fantasy in 1888. Behind an iron fence salvaged from the playground of one of Chicago's oldest public schools sits the white limestone structure. Essentially Queen Anne in design, it was a bit pricier to construct than most of the neighboring buildings. The rusticated facade features columns of granite, heavily polished to look like marble, and a turret that rests on a shell-shaped base. The stonework on the second-floor balcony follows a checkerboard pattern, and the

handrails are scrolled with a motif of oak leaves. That cornice is not fabricated with stone but with sheet metal, a cost and fire-safety compromise employed on many homes in the area.

On the corner is the former:

5. **Serbian Eastern Orthodox Church.** This cream-colored building, which occupies the triangular point where Schiller intersects with Evergreen Avenue, is still in service to religion. Two gospel congregations, one in English, the other Spanish, share the church.

At this corner, double back behind the church on Evergreen and stop in front of:

6. **1958 W. Evergreen Ave.** The house is interesting for much of its exterior, including the stonework—like the griffin in the keystone on the first floor, the urn with its sunflower on the second floor, and the bas-relief of little cupids. More interesting is the fact that novelist Nelson Algren (1909–81) lived in a third-floor apartment from 1959 to 1975. Algren today is best remembered for his two dark novels of the urban semiunderworld, *A Walk on the Wild Side* and *The Man with the Golden Arm* (which was set near here, around Division and Milwaukee), and for his tough but lyrical prose poem, *Chicago: City on the Make*. A sidewalk marker provides further information on the author's life and work.

The next stop is optional, for it takes us off the path of this tour. Still, the destination and the identity of one former occupant justify the digression. At the corner of Evergreen and Damen avenues, turn left and head south one block to Potomac. Turn right and walk west for a block and a half, stopping at 2132 W. Potomac, the:

7. **Home of the Spies Family.** At ten o'clock on the morning of November 13, 1887, the coffin of August Spies was loaded onto a wagon. Some sources claim that as many as one million onlookers witnessed the funeral procession as it followed Milwaukee Avenue toward the downtown train station. Spies, a German-born leader of the Chicago trade-union movement and editor of the newspaper, *Arbeiter-Zeitung,* was one of four men who

had been hanged two days earlier in what is now regarded as one of the greatest miscarriages of justice in American history, the execution of the Haymarket martyrs.

From here, the cortege wound through the Wicker Park neighborhood, down Damen Avenue to Evergreen Avenue, and over to Milwaukee Avenue. It ultimately picked up the remains of four other Haymarket codefendants, three of whom had suffered the same grim fate as Spies; the other allegedly committed suicide on the day prior to his scheduled execution.

Return now to Damen Avenue and Schiller Street; across from the southern end of the park at 2009 W. Schiller St. is the:

8. **Pritzker School.** The school bears the name of A. N. Pritzker, the son of a Russian immigrant, who grew up in the neighborhood and graduated from this institution when it was the Wicker Park School (his family went on to make big bucks with the Hyatt hotel chain). When the Chicago School Board cut the school's funds for after-school programs, Pritzker set up a foundation to fund activities and brought celebrities like Ernie Banks and the Harlem Globetrotters with him when he visited his alma mater. In a break with Chicago School Board regulations, the community was allowed to honor Pritzker by renaming the school for him while he was still living.

Continue west along Schiller Street to North Hoyne Avenue, one of the first paved streets in the city. People came from miles around to roller skate on Sunday afternoons. Hoyne Avenue from Evergreen Avenue to North Avenue is known as Beer Baron Row. Wealthy merchants built most of the fine homes here during the 1880s and 1890s. Turn right, stopping at:

9. **1407 N. Hoyne Ave.** Built by German wine and beer merchant John H. Rapp in 1880, this was the largest single-family estate in Wicker Park. The coach house, behind the mansion at 2044 W. Schiller St., is now a separate residence. This was not a happy home. Mrs. Rapp went insane, a son was convicted of embezzlement, and Rapp was murdered by his female bookkeeper. The home itself is of Second Empire style, with a large, curbed mansard roof. The wrought-iron fence is original and defines the

boundaries of the original grounds. In 1920 the estate was sold and converted into four flats. In the neighborhood, this place is often referred to as the Goldblatt or Wieboldt Mansion, though no one from either of those great Chicago mercantile families—who were residents of Wicker Park—ever lived here.

Our next point of interest is:

10. **1417 N. Hoyne Ave.** This appealingly overgrown property once belonged to Carl Wernecke, who built it in 1879. The rolling landscape was created to simulate an asymmetrical meadow. The house is Italianate in style and has unusually high windows on the first floor. Note the richly tooled woodwork on the side porch, especially the columns; this appendage was not used as an entryway but strictly for gazing upon the splendors of the garden in bloom.

Across the street at **1426 N. Hoyne Ave.** is a good example of a worker's cottage, and a reminder that in these old immigrant neighborhoods, artisans and their patrons often lived side by side.

The next house down is:

11. **1427 N. Hoyne Ave.** The former home of a Norwegian furniture manufacturer, built in the late 1880s, this house typifies a phenomenon in the construction business of this era, when homes were designed piecemeal from a variety of pattern books. Many elements in eclectic homes of this type were simply ordered prefab. This house is primarily Romanesque, but incorporates other elements, such as Queen Anne. There is nothing prefab about the workmanship on the Scandinavian woodworker's porch, however. The bay of the porch is a combination of wood and pressed metal, a technique that came into fashion after the Great Fire of 1871.

On the next corner, at Le Moyne Street and Hoyne Avenue, is the:

12. **Wicker Park Lutheran Church.** Quaintly known as "the church with a heart in the heart of Chicago," it is also the city's oldest permanent Lutheran church. The building was modeled from plans of Holy Trinity Church in Caen, France, dating from the 12th century. The stone for

this Romanesque structure was recycled from a demolished bawdy house on South Michigan Avenue. To one of his scandalized parishioners, the pastor remarked that the building material "has served the devil long enough; now let it serve the Lord."

Now walk on to:

13. **1520 N. Hoyne Ave.** A lumber merchant named Henry Grusendorf built this estate spanning two city lots in 1887. French Empire in design, the house—now containing two apartments—retains many of its original features, including four fireplaces. Inside, the ceilings rise to almost 14 feet and are decorated with ornate plasterwork and moldings. Note the double-gabled "queen" porch, the jeweled and stained-glass windows, and especially the anatomical forms supporting the banisters on the front stairs—cast-iron replicas of human hands. This is one of the few grand homes in Wicker Park that was never converted into a rooming house.

Directly across the street is:

14. **1521 N. Hoyne Ave.** War profiteering, according to some, allowed Isaac Waixel to build this residence (ca. 1890) after he grossed a cool $20 million by selling beef to the federal government during the Civil War. Another faction of historico-architects claims a more prosaic origin for this home: the hands of the German master chairmaker, later manufacturing executive, Adolph Borgmeier. By general agreement, the fetching workmanship, both inside and outside, was Borgmeier's. The building's design combines elements of Queen Anne and Romanesque styles, while the metal trim is rife with decorative symbols: rosettes, flowers, scrolls, dentils, and scrolled Ionic columns in relief on the dormer. Note also the likeness of a woman carved into the exterior, a typical embellishment on German-built houses.

Across the alley was the site of the original Schlitz Mansion, demolished in the 1920s to make room for the utilitarian yellow-brick apartment building you see before you. The beer magnate once owned the entire block from Pierce Avenue to Damen Avenue. He later moved his brewery to Milwaukee. Next we move across the street to:

15. **1530 N. Hoyne Ave.** Noted more for its former residents than its architecture, this home was once occupied by William Leger, a newspaperman and Democratic Party activist who coined the phrase "Beer Baron Row." Leger rose from the ad department of a German-language daily to become president of two local brewing companies. It was later the home of German architect Hermann Gaul, who designed many Chicago churches, including St. Michael's, St. Benedict's, St. Matthias, and St. Raphael. Gaul lived here from 1912 to 1939 with his wife and their 10 children.

   The corner of Pierce and Hoyne was, in its day, one of the most fashionable addresses in the city. Cross Pierce Avenue and continue on the left side of the street to:

16. **1558 N. Hoyne Ave.** The building permit for this Queen Anne–style home was issued in 1877, making it one of the oldest homes in this area. It was built for C. Hermann Plautz, founder (in 1861) of the Chicago Drug and Chemical Company, president of the Northwestern Brewing Company, and later city treasurer of Chicago. Ever conscious of the Chicago Fire, the builders created all the decorative trim on both towers, the cornices, and the conservatory of the south side from ornamental pressed metal. The seemingly misplaced cannon in the front yard is a relic of the years (1927–72) when the building housed the local American Legion, which used the 800-square-foot former living room as a meeting hall. The landscaping followed an 1870 Victorian garden book, and the garden contains a weeping juniper and a Norway dwarf spruce.

   Now return to Pierce Avenue and walk west to:

17. **2118 W. Pierce Ave.** This French château–style home with neoclassical elements was built for Theodore Noel, a drug company executive, in 1903. The dormer is Gothic Revival; the pineapple frieze is a symbol of hospitality. The slate sidewalk in front of the house is original.

   Two doors down is:

18. **2134 W. Pierce Ave.** Also vaguely French château, this structure was constructed in 1903 for Theodore's brother

Joseph Noel, a banker, by the same team who built no. 2118. Notable details on the facade are the twisting bands, or *guilloche* pattern, that resolve the framing and the bay-leaf garland molding hanging from the second story. For some time during the 1940s, the house served as a residence for a local settlement house (see Stop 32, below). Today, it contains two apartments.

Across the street is 2137 W. Pierce Ave., the:

19. **Hermann Weinhardt House.** This well-preserved gem (1888) is one of the highlights of the tour. You'll need no further evidence that German culture does not entirely fall within the tradition of the West once you have taken in the oriental fantasy manifested by the outline of this extraordinary structure. Weinhardt was a manufacturer and a West Park Commissioner. One critic referred to his creation as a "Victorian gingerbread design"; in truth, the house defies association with any genre.

The charm is in the whole, but among the notable details are the elaborate balcony of carved wood facing east, and the unusual juxtaposition of green stone and redbrick limestone, which creates a singular effect around the large front window. This lot is sizable and was once flooded annually for ice-skating. The core of the house, without the porches, is quite narrow, like the neighboring workers' cottages. Its three stories, however, sit astride an English basement, where the kitchen is still in use for everyday cooking.

Of interest both historically and architecturally is 2138 W. Pierce Ave., the:

20. **Hans D. Runge House.** Runge was treasurer of the Wolf Brothers Wood Milling Company. His home, built in 1884, is considered one of the best surviving examples in the area of the Eastlake style of ornamentation of porch posts, balusters, railings, and so forth. The style takes its name from Charles Locke Eastlake, a 19th-century English interior designer. As to the overall design, various styles have been suggested: Swiss chalet, Viennese cottage, and carpenter's steamboat. Elaborate wood-carving characterizes the house inside and out; among the unique designs are the Masonic symbols flanking the pair of

dragon heads under the rounded arch. A well-heeled local banker and politician, John F. Smulski, acquired the house in 1902, which was about the time many Poles were moving into the neighborhood. Smulski committed suicide here after the stock market crash in 1929, and the house served for a time as the Polish consulate. On one memorable occasion in the 1930s, the great pianist—and onetime prime minister of Poland for a brief span after World War I—Ignacy Paderewski treated the neighborhood to a concert from the upper level of the elegant two-story front porch. The house's current owners appear to be giving it some tender loving care, keeping the intricate trim freshly painted.

Across the street is:

21. **2141 W. Pierce Ave.** The prelate of Chicago's Ukrainian Church occupied this home from 1954 to 1971, as the Eastern Cross atop the roof still testifies. The early Queen Anne structure was originally built for Theodore Daniel Juergens, whose Horatio Alger life saw him climb from the jobs of telegraph operator, sign painter, and decorator to the presidency of the American Varnish Company. Gargoyle fans will enjoy the grotesque figures leering down from above the original finial and at the corners of the house. Facing the garden on the east side is the first-floor conservatory; the third floor once held a ballroom.

An interesting relic of the preautomotive world remains at curbside before:

22. **2150 W. Pierce Ave.** Visitors used the stepping stone near the driveway when they descended from a horse and carriage at the curb. The inscription "J. C. Horn" preserves the name of the original owner, a furniture manufacturer and president of the Horn Bros. Manufacturing Company.

This house is just one of several faithful examples of the once-popular rusticated Romanesque look. Among the houses of this genre nearby are nos. 2146 and 2156. The latter was home to another rag-to-riches success story, August Lempke, a peddler who became vice president of a coal company and state fish commissioner.

The large building across the street is now a nursing home. Until 1960, it was a branch of the:

23. **Eleanor Club.** These were respectable dormitories for single working women. In the early years, residents received room plus breakfast and dinner for $6.50 a week. The commodious living conditions included a variety of common spaces, such as homelike parlors and living rooms, a roof garden, sleeping porch, sewing room, library, and laundry.

Turn right onto Leavitt Street and walk to North Avenue. Making a short diversion to the west (left), the red-brick building on the south side of the street at 2215 W. North Ave. is the former:

24. **St. Paul's Lutheran Church.** The original congregation was founded in 1873, and this building went up almost 20 years later. Services were in Norwegian until 1903. The church, now home to an interdenominational congregation, is typically closed during the week; if the building happens to be open, you'd see an interior of elaborate woodwork carved to create the illusion of being in an ark. The first pipe organ installed by the Austin Company in Chicago was built here in 1906.

Cross North Avenue and continue up Leavitt Street to Concord Place. The lots here are smaller because this area was developed later, when land was already at a premium; most of the newcomers then were Scandinavians rather than Germans. One novelty not to be missed is:

25. **1630 N. Leavitt St.** This clapboard farmhouse was moved to this site in 1914. To spruce up the structure, the porch, bays, and leaded glass were added at this location.

Up the block toward Caton Street is:

26. **1646 N. Leavitt St.** This home was built for Fred A. Miller in 1897. With its fine stonework, it represents the beaux arts style of architecture. Over the entrance is an unusual oval window of beveled glass; the beaded molding surrounding the door is also worthy of note. The house has been restored in recent years, which was not a cheap proposition. The restoration of the cornice alone was said to cost $16,000.

Many of the houses on Caton Street, one of the city's most unusual streets, were built in the early 1890s by the same architectural firm, Faber and Pagels, each according to a different fantasy and style. Turn right on Caton and walk toward Milwaukee Avenue; the numbers go in descending order. The first house of interest is:

27. **2156 W. Caton St.** An import-export entrepreneur, Ole Thorpe, built this and the three houses adjacent to it around 1892. At the time, his project was known as the Thorpe subdivision. This house is described as a German Burgher manse, though its fireplace is adorned with the crest of Norway. There's also a terrazzo floor in the basement-level ballroom. On the outside, the most obvious feature is the heavy domed turret rising from the flared and rusticated foundations. There are also many stained-glass windows, which the owners have illuminated, including one on the side topped with a half-moon lunette. And don't miss the sunburst design over the door on the second-story porch.

   Continuing a few steps to the east, we come to:

28. **2152 W. Caton St.** The original owner of this 1891 home was a livery contractor named Max Tauber. He had the largest stable operation in the city and was also a crony of the mayor's. The house was described as Renaissance, while the melodrama enfolding within its walls during Tauber's tenure was decidedly Byzantine, with an American twist. Upon hearing the erroneous news that Max had died in a fire at work, his first wife succumbed to a heart attack. Max took a new wife in the 1920s, and then lost his shirt in the stock market crash of 1929. Eschewing the option of declaring bankruptcy, he formed a partnership in banking with his Pierce Avenue neighbor Joseph Noel, recouped his fortunes, and repaid his debts. Soon thereafter, in the 1930s, he murdered his second wife and took his own life. The house was then converted into a rooming house. Today it's a single-family home.

   Stay on this side of the street and move to:

29. **2142 W. Caton St.** Before you is a 14-room mansion, one of the most elegant homes on the street. The

workmanship, both inside and out, is highly detailed. A facade of rusticated pink sandstone at street level transforms into one of textured brick on the upper stories. A free-standing Romanesque column supports the turret, with its original spike finial.

The cornice is of pressed metal and the columns of polished granite. The house has always been a single-family home, and many of the interior fixtures are original, as are the stained-glass windows, the woodwork, and all the hardware.

Crossing the street, walk back to:

30. **2145 W. Caton St.** Remember John F. Smulski from the Hans D. Runge House on Pierce Avenue (Stop 20, above)? This was his original home, when his father was the first publisher of a Polish-language newspaper in Chicago. Before losing his fortune and his life as a result of the 1929 stock market crash, Smulski too had been a partner with Joseph Noel in the Northwest Savings Bank. He was also a failed Republican candidate in the Chicago mayoral race of 1911.

Next door is:

31. **2147 W. Caton St.** William A. Thoresen commissioned this Classical Revival home, which was completed in 1906. The house is built of flat cut gray stone and trimmed entirely in metal. Thoresen, it seems, owned an architectural metals mill, and the products of his factory adorn much of the home's exterior; the interior is finished in tinwork, to include the domed ceiling in the dining room. The porch also has a tin ceiling. Note other examples of exterior ornamentation in metal, particularly the garlands of grapes and flowers. This house has the only flat roof on the block.

Retrace your steps along Caton and Leavitt to North Avenue and turn left. That large complex of buildings at 2150 W. North Ave. is:

32. **Association House of Chicago.** Related in spirit to the settlement house tradition, this institution, directed toward combating the effects of chronic poverty on immigrant women, was begun in 1899 by the YWCA. Jane

Addams, founder of the settlement house movement, laid the current building's cornerstone in 1905. Local businesses assumed financial support of Association House when men were admitted in 1910, and the YWCA chose to leave. Today Association House provides a range of social-service programs, including child welfare, mental health, and employment and training. Take note of the mural and mosaic on the building's east side, both the works of neighborhood youth participating in a summer art program.

At the next intersection, look north along Hoyne Avenue toward the southeast corner of Concord. The building at **1617–1619 N. Hoyne Ave.,** behind the recycling station, was once the neighborhood livery stable, where locals stored their carriages and boarded their horses. The brick building, which became a factory when the horse and buggy went out, has since been converted to condos. The final stop on our tour is at 2039 W. North Ave., a building that until recently housed the:

33. **Luxor Baths.** This old immigrant spa—also known as the North Avenue Baths—dates to the 1920s; a reminder of a vanishing institution, the public bath, it has been transformed into—what else?—a dozen apartments for yuppies. There is even a trendy Asian-fusion restaurant, Spring, on the ground floor. The original terra-cotta facade bears a nautical motif that gleams as it hasn't in years. The building reputedly was once a haven for businesspeople, politicos, and other wheeler-dealers. According to local legend, it might even have been a favorite mob hangout.

At the next corner, you return to the three-road intersection where the tour began. The tall building is the **Northwest Tower,** one of the finest examples of Art Deco design in Chicago, constructed by the downtown architectural firm of Perkins and Chatten in 1929. At the time the 12-story building opened, it was the tallest structure outside downtown. "Around the Coyote," a neighborhood art festival held in early September, is named for the building that some in Wicker Park seem to think looks like a wolf baying at the moon.

Winding Down   To the north on Damen Avenue are a number of restaurants and cafes. For a detour with a decidedly Italian flavor, walk a block and a half north to **Caffe de Luca,** 1721 N. Damen Ave. (☎ **773/ 342-6000**), where the owners have reproduced the small town of Cindente, Italy. The menu is simple, with Italian sodas, pastries, and coffee available to go. In the summer, you can sit outside and enjoy a scoop or two of gelato.

· Walking Tour 9 ·

Oak Park

Start: Frank Lloyd Wright Home and Studio, 951 Chicago Ave., Oak Park (☎ 708/848-1976). Visit www.wrightplus.org for complete tour information.

Public Transportation: A good option is the Metra commuter line. Board the train at North Western station (officially the Ogilvie Transportation Center) at Madison and Canal in downtown Chicago. Get off at the Oak Park/Marion Street station. The trip takes about 20 minutes.

The westbound Green line (Lake St.) elevated train also stops in Oak Park, at Oak Park Avenue, and at Harlem Avenue, the end of the line.

Finish: Hemingway Birthplace, 339 N. Oak Park Ave.

Time: 2 to 3 hours.

Best Times: If you want to follow this itinerary to the letter, coordinate your start with the times of scheduled tours at the two most important sights in Oak Park, the Wright Home and Studio and Unity Temple. Home and Studio tours begin Monday to Friday at 11am, 1pm, and 3pm; Saturday and Sunday every 15 minutes from 11am to 3:30pm. The schedule for visiting Unity Temple is listed under Stop 16 of this tour. There are no self-guided tours at the Wright Home and Studio; you must purchase a ticket at the attached Ginkgo Tree Bookshop and take a scheduled tour. Try to arrive 15 minutes in advance of the time you've selected; this guided portion of the tour lasts approximately 45 minutes.

Worst Times: Whenever the Wright Home and Studio or Unity Temple aren't open to the public, or when the weather is bad.

Visitor Information: The Oak Park Visitors Center, Stop 14 on the tour, is on Forest Avenue.

A mill owner with the colorful name of Kettlestrings settled Oak Park in the early 1830s, but the area didn't really begin to develop until after the Great Fire of 1871. Today Oak Park Village is a residential suburb of Chicago, but it is proud to remain a separate municipal entity, just outside the city limits, roughly 10 miles from downtown.

Oak Park's most famous native son was Ernest Hemingway, whose birthplace (the home of his maternal grandfather) has been converted into a museum. The village is best known, however, as the great showcase of Frank Lloyd Wright's earliest architectural achievements. It contains some 2 dozen homes and buildings commissioned by his friends and neighbors. Many of these homes are in Oak Park's historic district, which forms the core of this excursion. The area abounds not only with examples of Wright's Prairie School architecture, but with magnificent works in the Victorian, Stick, and Italianate styles, executed by Wright's contemporaries.

One of Wright's most celebrated creations, Unity Temple, is also here. He designed and built the church for his own Unitarian congregation.

• • • • • • • • • • • • • • • • •

Starting Out Petersen's, 1100 W. Chicago Ave. (☎ 708/386-6131), specializes in family dining and a wide selection of desserts, including an old-fashioned ice cream parlor that is a long-time Chicago-area favorite. It's a few short blocks from the Home and Studio. If you'd like to start your tour with a pastry and a cup of take-out coffee, Petersen's is the place. (Finish up before the house tour begins.)

Oak Park

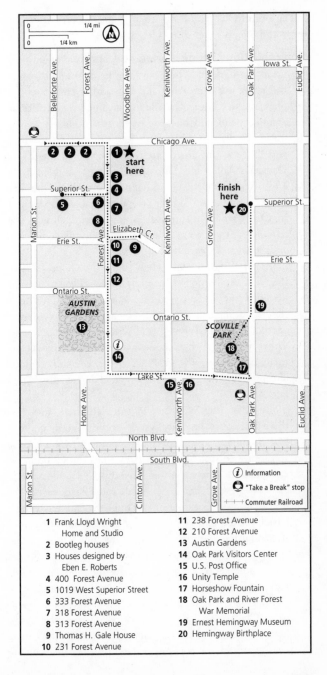

1 Frank Lloyd Wright
   Home and Studio
2 Bootleg houses
3 Houses designed by
   Eben E. Roberts
4 400 Forest Avenue
5 1019 West Superior Street
6 333 Forest Avenue
7 318 Forest Avenue
8 313 Forest Avenue
9 Thomas H. Gale House
10 231 Forest Avenue

11 238 Forest Avenue
12 210 Forest Avenue
13 Austin Gardens
14 Oak Park Visitors Center
15 U.S. Post Office
16 Unity Temple
17 Horseshow Fountain
18 Oak Park and River Forest
   War Memorial
19 Ernest Hemingway Museum
20 Hemingway Birthplace

A tour of Oak Park is essentially a tour of Wright's architectural legacy and should begin at the:

1. **Frank Lloyd Wright Home and Studio.** Wright grew
up in Richland, a Wisconsin farming community where
his father was a preacher and his mother taught school.
He came to Chicago in 1887 and joined the firm of an
architect who had once designed two buildings for an
uncle who lived in Hyde Park. Later that year, the young
and largely untrained architect began to work for
Dankmar Adler and Louis Sullivan as a draftsman. In
1889, Wright married, and Sullivan lent Wright (by then
his chief draftsman) $5,000 to purchase land for a home
in Oak Park. The original "shingle-style" cottage was
completed that year; it underwent modifications and
additions over a period of 2 decades.

As the Wrights' family grew, so did their house. At first
the two-story home was relatively small—a few beautifully
designed but compact rooms organized around a central
fireplace and partly surrounded by a geometrically shaped
veranda that contained seeds of Wright's later Prairie style.
Other features, such as the wide horizontal window case-
ment dominating the gable facade on the second floor,
also prefigure the idiom that would characterize Wright's
later work.

By 1894, the Wrights had three children (they had
three more over the next 9 years), and the family quarters
had become cramped. Wright responded by building a
spacious two-story addition. On the ground floor, he
expanded the kitchen into a large dining room and relocated the new kitchen and a maid's room at the rear of the
house. Above this extension, he built the children a large,
barrel-vaulted playroom, which has been described as "a
structural tour de force . . . a gymnasium, kindergarten,
concert hall, and theater all in one." Wright's former
home office and studio, on the second floor above the
entrance, was partitioned into girls' and boys' dormitories.

By 1898, Wright had relinquished his offices in downtown Chicago and attached a workshop complex to his
home. It included a two-story octagonal studio with a
central atrium, a reception area and private office, and an

octagonal library. By this time, Wright had fully conceptualized the key elements of his Prairie-style architecture, and his spectacular workspace incorporated many of these innovations.

To fully appreciate the scope and beauty of Wright's accomplishments here, I strongly advise that you take the tour of the interior. The organization that exercises stewardship over this remarkable shrine to the Great American Architect is the Frank Lloyd Wright Home and Studio Foundation. Over a 12-year period ending in 1986, the foundation oversaw a massive restoration of the Home and Studio, returning it to its general appearance in 1909, when Wright left for Europe with the wife of a client under a cloud of social disapproval. Tours are offered weekdays at 11am, 1pm, and 3pm, and on weekends every 20 minutes between 11am and 3:30pm; admission is $9 for adults, $7 for children 7 to 18.

Wright owned the home until 1925, when he sold it, and his family vacated the premises. By then the complex had undergone many more significant transformations. It had fallen into ruinous condition by the time it was purchased for preservation. The buildings were restored to their appearance during the architect's productive tenure here, where within 11 years he completed 125 projects—over a quarter of his life's work.

When you exit the Frank Lloyd Wright Home and Studio, cross Forest Avenue and walk west along Chicago Avenue to the cluster of:

2. **Bootleg houses.** Frank Lloyd Wright designed and built these homes, nos. 1019, 1027, and 1031 Chicago Ave., between 1892 and 1893, while he was still employed by Adler and Sullivan. Under the terms of his contract, Wright was not permitted to work outside the firm. Sullivan discovered his moonlighting in 1893, causing a permanent rift between the men, and leading Wright to leave the firm and take up practice on his own.

With each of these houses, Wright worked essentially in a Victorian medium that he would ultimately come to despise. Nonetheless, these structures already reflect Wright's mastery over the architectural skills that enhanced his cherished vision of simple home comforts.

Return to Forest Avenue and turn right, walking away from Chicago Avenue to:

3. **Houses designed by Eben E. Roberts.** Roberts was another popular Oak Park architect and a late contemporary of Frank Lloyd Wright's. He designed and executed more than 200 houses during his productive career and worked in every style. No. 426 Forest Ave. (1897) is an early Roberts house in the popular Queen Anne style. With 422 Forest Ave. (1900), Roberts began to break with Victorian tradition and pioneer the low, boxy configuration that characterized many of his later houses. His own experiment with the idiom of the Prairie School is visible in another of his Forest Avenue homes, no. 415.

Our first sample of Wright's architecture on this block is:

4. **400 Forest Ave.** This house, built for Dr. William H. Copeland in 1894, is by no means typical of Wright's work in Oak Park. Perhaps the good doctor had ideas of his own, and the young architect simply chose to accommodate him. The house, however, does possess the unmistakable "horizontality" of Prairie School architecture.

To see architect Eben E. Roberts's home, take a brief digression west, along the south side of Superior, the first cross street, to:

5. **1019 W. Superior.** The home (1911) is remarkable for its lack of pretense in a neighborhood where architectural one-upmanship was obviously the fashion. If anything, the house appears to be a pattern for the cookie-cutter homes that proliferated in suburbs throughout the country after World War II.

Return to Forest Avenue and walk to the house on the corner:

6. **333 Forest Ave.** This Frank Lloyd Wright creation was built in 1895 for Nathan G. Moore, who enjoined the architect to "give me something Elizabethan." Wright, to be sure, was almost as ambivalent about this Tudor styling as he was about the nonfunctional excesses of ornamentation that he associated with anything in the Victorian mode. Commenting late in life in his memoirs, he wryly

noted that "anyone could get a rise out of me by admiring that essay in English half-timber. They all liked it, and I could have gone on unnaturally building them for the rest of my natural life." In 1922, when a fire burned the house down to its first story, Wright was asked to supervise the remodeling. The second time around, Wright departed from the original Tudor genre, adding such spectacular details as the gothic bay, the cantilevered porch roof, and the Mayan trim.

Turn around and look across the street, where the visual fare begins to improve exponentially with our next stopping point:

7. **318 Forest Ave.,** the Arthur B. Heurtley House (1902). This is something of a fine first draft for Robie House, the Hyde Park home Wright completed 7 years later, which today is viewed as his residential masterpiece. To the lay observer, the two homes have much in common. They are both long and low, with walls of richly decorated horizontal windows. Each lies partially hidden behind a brick wall; the Heurtley House's wall rises almost to the roofline, allowing a seemingly narrow space on the second story for a band of glass running the length of the eaves.

The effect is of a highly stylized battlement lined with glittering gun ports. The front door, beneath a formal archway, remains hidden from view. It suggests both the sanctity of domestic privacy and the illusion of entering one's residence not directly into the static parlor, but by way of the door yard, the normal place for comings and goings in an active home. This hidden entryway, borrowed from the work of H. H. Richardson by way of Louis Sullivan, would become a trademark of Wright's architecture.

Across the street we next come to:

8. **313 Forest Ave.** Here's a house that predates Wright's arrival in Oak Park by several years. Nathan G. Moore called upon Wright to remodel it between 1900 and 1906. Moore bought this originally Stick-style frame house for his daughter, Mary. The house was moved from its foundation on the lot and turned 90° so its broad front would face Forest Avenue.

Wright's remodeling was so radical that little of the appearance of the original house remains. One of the structure's most striking features is the pagoda roof, echoed in the caps over the porch and the third-story dormer.

That little building in the yard began its life as a ticket booth at the 1893 World's Columbian Exposition in Chicago.

Here we will make another brief detour, turning left onto Elizabeth Ct., the only curved street in Oak Park. At 6 Elizabeth Ct. is the:

9. **Thomas H. Gale House.** This 1909 construction has that quintessential Frank Lloyd Wright look. It is a fore-runner to Fallingwater, the home Wright built in Bear Run, Pennsylvania, and one major source of the narrow image the world has of the architect's legacy. (Another is New York City's somewhat grotesque and surrealistic Guggenheim Museum.) Seen as a singular creation with-out reference to the Wright stereotype, especially here in Oak Park where so many neighboring homes have that doily-like look of respectability, this house provides a pleasant jolt to the visual senses. The double porches, for example, project something latently aggressive, as if a ship's conning tower were ready to bear down on you (but for the fact that its superstructure and hull are beneath street level).

Return now to Forest Avenue and pause before one of the oldest houses in the village:

10. **231 Forest Ave.** This simple two-story clapboard is the pattern of Oak Park's earliest dwellings, built around 1873. Often, cottages like this were remodeled to the point where the renovation transformed the simplicity of the original design. Others were simply moved to neigh-borhoods where the real estate was less pricey.

A case in point of a modest cottage being remodeled beyond recognition is:

11. **238 Forest Ave.,** known as the Peter Beachy House. One of Wright's sisters lived here during the 1930s and '40s. Like the home at 333 Forest Ave., this example of

Wright and company's handiwork has the look of a big box, with various surface forms added to soften the structure's symmetry. Four materials—limestone, brick, plaster, and wood trim—lend depth and texture to the facade. Notice that the lot this house sits on is unusually deep.

A few steps down the block is:

12. **210 Forest Ave.** Here at the Frank W. Thomas House, we return to the horizontal layout that produced such pleasant results in the hands of the master modernist, who saw in this form an affirmation of the human link to nature. This 1901 construction is considered Wright's first contribution to the Prairie School of architecture (although he had already built a house with similar dimensions in his home state of Wisconsin). Some of the characteristic Prairie architecture features in the Thomas House are the flat, hipped roof—used to eliminate wasted attic space—and the small windows on the second floor, which here suggest a Chinese influence. Also, the house has no basement, which Wright came to consider "unwholesome." Here Wright also employed the shielded entryway; the rounded portal appears to shelter a front door, but it leads to one at the top of a concealed stairway.

Across the street from the Thomas House is:

13. **Austin Gardens.** This attractive green space is named for one of Oak Park's original teetotaling settlers, Henry W. Austin. For the most part, Oak Park remains "dry" to this day, though village statutes do allow local restaurants to serve alcoholic beverages. Note the bust of Frank Lloyd Wright at the Forest Avenue entrance to the park.

Beyond the park, on the left before you get to Lake Street, at 158 Forest Ave., is the:

14. **Oak Park Visitors Center** (☎ 708/848-1500; www. visitoakpark.com). The staff can answer any questions about local orientation. There are clean restrooms and items for sale, including maps, guidebooks, postcards, souvenirs, and tour tickets. Adjacent to the facility is a parking lot. The center is open daily from 10am to 5pm (until 4pm in winter).

Continue to Lake Street, turn left, and cross the street. Walk toward the intersection of Kenilworth Avenue, and at the side entrance nearest you, go inside the:

15. **U.S. Post Office.** This is one of those massive public buildings worth examining more closely for several reasons. For one, the Art Deco interior is beautifully appointed and impeccably maintained. There are several murals in the romantic Americana vein, and the wrought-iron grillwork surrounding the portals is an amusing tableau of figures and vehicles used over the years for mail delivery.

Exit the post office at the far end of the building onto Kenilworth Avenue. Across the street at 875 Lake St. is a National Historic Landmark building that many consider Frank Lloyd Wright's perfect creation. If you have a camera with you, the best place to frame the Unity Temple is from the rear steps of the post office. So take your pictures before crossing over to:

16. **Unity Temple.** "The reality of the building," said Wright, "is the space within." Perhaps nowhere else in the architect's work is that more true than in this extraordinarily unconventional house of worship. Called upon by his congregation to replace the old church, which had burned to the ground, Wright submitted his plan for the "temple" in 1905.

His choice of concrete was pragmatic; he selected building materials with an eye toward economy, given the limited funds available for the project. It is not surprising, therefore, that on an initial, cursory examination, this massive block of concrete may seem off-putting, even ugly. But a closer look will reveal that the exterior of Wright's "little jewel" is not without grace in either form or detail. The outline of the building, especially from the side, is a sight of rare structural beauty. And much of the decorative detail serves some functional purpose as well: The hollow columns contain the original heating ducts, the roof's waffle construction allows the infiltration of natural light, and so forth.

The interior of the temple, within the actual chapel, is where Wright simultaneously delivers his knockout blow to the mind's eye and the aesthetic senses. Here Wright, in his lifelong crusade against Victorian sentimentality, offers the most convincing evidence that beauty is not synonymous with cuteness, no matter how complex in appearance. The lines, the forms, the colors, and the composition within this singular space could not be more spare and restrained. And yet the effect is monumental, a tribute to the transcendental deism of Thoreau and Emerson. Here one does not bow before the supernatural, but stands erect with full confidence in the human spirit and all its unfulfilled potential. Wright was well aware from the beginning of how daring a statement this work articulated; he also felt considerable apprehension and failed to attend the inaugural service because he was not at all certain of how his fellow congregants would react.

You need a ticket to enter Unity Temple, and you may choose an accompanied or self-guided tour, depending on the day of your visit. In either case, expert docents provide a suitably detailed account of each architectural twist and turn Wright employed in the church. Unity Temple is open 10:30am to 4:30pm weekdays and 1 to 4pm weekends. Admission costs $6, and guided tours are available Saturday and Sunday at 1, 2, and 3pm for no extra charge. For more information, call ☎ **708/383-8873.**

Cross Lake Street, follow it past the Oak Park Public Library, and walk along Scoville Park toward Oak Park Avenue. At the southeast corner of the park is:

17. **Horseshow Fountain.** This park adornment is a re-creation of a fountain designed in 1909. It's unclear who did the designing—sculptor Richard Bock, his friend and associate Frank Lloyd Wright, or a mix of both men's ideas. The outcome was certainly clever: a fountain that allowed humans to drink at the highest level and horses and dogs to drink below.

Now walk toward the center of the park until you come to the:

18. **Oak Park and River Forest War Memorial.** This monument was erected in 1925 in tribute to World War I service personnel from surrounding communities. On the southeast side of the base is the name of Ernest Hemingway.

    Walk north through the park until you reach Oak Park Avenue at Ontario Street. At 200 N. Oak Park Ave., you may wish to pay a brief visit to the:

19. **Ernest Hemingway Museum** (☎ 708/848-2222; www.hemingway.org). Oak Park has only recently begun to rally around the memory of its Nobel and Pulitzer prize–winning native son, Ernest Hemingway. A portion of the ground floor of this former church, now the Oak Park Arts Center, is given over to a small but interesting display of Hemingway memorabilia. It offers several short video presentations, including one that sheds considerable light on Hemingway's time in Oak Park, where he spent the first 18 years of his life; it's particularly good on the writer's high school experiences.

    The museum's hours are limited: Both the museum and birthplace house (see below) are open Thursday, Friday and Sunday from 1 to 5pm and Saturday from 10am to 5pm; additionally, the house is open Wednesday from 1 to 5pm. A special admission price ($7 for adults, $5.50 for students and seniors) covers both museums.

    To see where Hemingway was born, continue up the block to 339 N. Oak Park Ave., the:

20. **Hemingway Birthplace.** On July 21, 1899, in the home of his maternal grandparents, the author of several great American novels was born. A local foundation recently bought the home to serve as a museum; a thorough renovation was completed in 1999, the centennial of the writer's birth, and the house now reflects its appearance during Hemingway's boyhood. Hemingway's actual boyhood home, still privately owned, is several blocks from here, not far from the Wright Home and Studio, at 600 N. Kenilworth Ave.

    Our tour of Oak Park ends here. You may easily walk back to the train station along Lake Street, or take a break before returning to Chicago at any one of several restaurants on Oak Park Avenue.

Winding Down   The restaurants on this block offer a variety of cuisines. If you want to keep it simple, try **Erik's Delicatessen,** 107 N. Oak Park Ave. (☎ **708/ 848-8805**), where sandwiches and a salad bar top the menu.

Hyde Park

Start: 53rd Street and Lake Park Avenue, across from the 53rd Street stop of the Metra train.

Public Transportation: Take the Metra, Chicago's suburban train line, from one of two downtown locations, Randolph at Michigan Avenue or Van Buren at LaSalle Street. Be sure you board the Metra Electric (still sometimes called by its former name, the Illinois Central or IC) train that makes all stops; the ride to 53rd Street takes about 15 minutes. The no. 6 Jeffrey Express bus, which you can pick up at designated stops in the Loop along State Street, runs much more frequently than the train. Drivers can leave their cars in a metered city lot at 53rd Street and Lake Park Avenue.

Finish: The Museum of Science and Industry in Jackson Park. If you like, from there you can walk back along the Metra tracks or reboard the train at the 59th Street/University of Chicago stop.

Time: 2 to 3 hours.

Best Time: Daily during daylight hours.

Worst Time: After dark.

Before the mid-1800s, the land now occupied by Hyde Park was sparsely settled.

Farmsteads, a roadhouse or two, an outlying estate belonging to a squire seeking pastoral relief from the foul odors and anarchy of the city: That was the landscape in an area located, by today's urban measure, a mere 50 or 60 city blocks from the southern bounds of contemporary downtown Chicago.

As an official entity, Hyde Park wasn't founded until 1853, when Paul Cornell, a young lawyer transplanted to the Midwest from New York, purchased 300 acres along the lakefront as a speculative real estate investment. Cornell's vision was to create a genteel haven near the city for gentlefolk of means who, like himself, made their livings as professionals and executives. He chose the name "Hyde Park" because he admired the Hudson River enclave of the same name; he hoped to replicate that kind of village on Lake Michigan.

Cornell's intention from the beginning was to attract a large institution that would provide a firm base for the local economy, but to keep heavy industry and manufacture at bay. To a large degree, Hyde Park's development has proceeded according to Cornell's plan. There have been bumps, but Hyde Park today remains a highly desirable residential neighborhood.

The institution Cornell dreamed of didn't materialize in Hyde Park until after his death. More than any other single factor, the establishment of the University of Chicago in 1890 made the fulfillment of his dream possible, even in the modified form it has assumed today. Hyde Park over the years has been buffeted by a succession of changing social realities: What was originally an elite neighborhood in the Age of Innocence has today become solidly middle class . . . and racially integrated. Ultimately, this social compromise in the area of race relations allowed Hyde Park to preserve its privileged ambience. By the end of World War II, the "white flight" to the suburbs was transforming neighborhoods all over Chicago's south side into racially homogeneous ghettos, as more and more African-Americans, displaced from rural communities in the South, fled north in search of blue-collar employment.

Hyde Park had retained its relatively uniform character as an affluent neighborhood until roughly the 1890s, when its Jackson Park was selected as the site for the World's Columbian Exposition. Against the wishes of the villagers, Hyde Park was then incorporated into the city of Chicago, and the massive development that accompanied the creation of the fair, plus ongoing advances and spread of public transportation, made it possible and convenient for middle- and working-class families to take up residence there.

By World War II, the village was in decline. The powerful presence of the University of Chicago, a massive injection of federal funds in the form of an urban-renewal program (which became a model for cities all over the country), and the decision to stop blocking middle-class African-Americans who wished to live there allowed Hyde Park to survive. Some of the poorest and most troubled neighborhoods in Chicago surround the serene, self-contained college town.

• • • • • • • • • • • • • • • •

Our tour begins just up the block from the train station at 1518 E. 53rd St., a famous Hyde Park institution:

1. **Valois.** Pronounced "va-*loys*" rather than "val-*wa*," this steam-table cafeteria originated as a workingman's eatery, but for years has also held a strong appeal among college students and other residents of varied social backgrounds. Shoulder to shoulder, you will see the bank president chowing down with the plumber.

   Turning right on Harper Avenue, our next stop is a complex of shops, studios, and restaurants with historic roots in Hyde Park's bohemian and avant-garde art movement:

2. **Harper Court.** Many of the buildings where a colorful constellation of Hyde Park artists once lived and had their studios were demolished during the massive urban renewal that took place here during the 1950s. As a form of compensation, Harper Court was built to "support artisans, craftsmen, and other services of special cultural or community significance." In general, rents at Harper Court would prove too high for struggling artists to afford. But four buildings were constructed around a pleasant public square and are occupied by retail tenants whose rents generate income that benefits some artists and the community in general. Among the specialty items featured in the boutiques are beads, goods from Africa,

Hyde Park

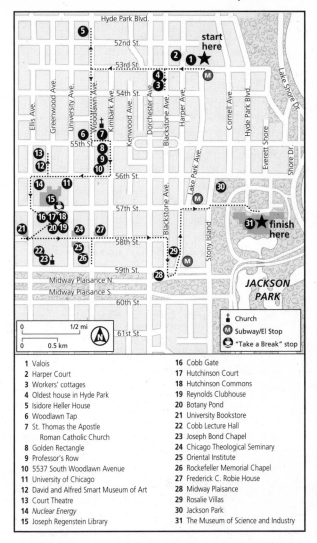

antiques, toys, health food, and CDs. There's also a gourmet carryout, a Caribbean restaurant, and a Southern-style restaurant.

Now cross 53rd Street and walk 1 block west before you turn left onto Blackstone Avenue. On the right (west) side of the street are a couple of:

3. **Workers' cottages.** These dwellings are typical of the homes built for workers who came to reside in Hyde Park, where they built, ran, and maintained the halls and attractions of the World's Columbian Exposition in the early 1890s.

    Return to 53rd Street and continue west along the south side of the street. Pause on the southeast corner of Dorchester Avenue and look across the parking lot to the:

4. **Oldest house in Hyde Park.** The lean-to or shedlike structure at the rear of the home at 5317 S. Dorchester Ave. was originally a board-and-batten-sided cottage, built by Henry C. Work in approximately 1859. Work was a very popular composer around the time of the Civil War, and a writer of temperance songs.

    Our next attraction takes us a bit off the main trail of our tour, but a detour and some extra walking are decidedly worthwhile when the quarry is a home built by Frank Lloyd Wright. Walk three blocks west to Woodlawn Avenue, turn right (north) at the shopping center, and continue just across 52nd Street to 5132 S. Woodlawn Ave., the:

5. **Isidore Heller House.** Here is living proof that by 1897, when this home was completed, Wright's reputation had already soared sufficiently in Chicago to attract important commissions outside Oak Park (until then, the incubator of his art). The remodeling and renovation projects he undertook for his Oak Park neighbors subjected him to the limits imposed by the existing structures. Wright already demonstrates with the Heller House a full command of the Prairie School idiom, so well fermented by that time in the minds of Chicago's Young Turk architects, with Wright very much in the forefront.

    For Wright, the flat roofs and exaggerated horizontality of the Heller House design were much more than an aesthetic statement; with a zealot's impatience, he was already aggressive about the business of trimming from the modern home all the useless space that smacked of Victorian excess, of form without function. Those bands of windows on Heller House, for example, not only were bold and attractive, but brought in an abundance of natural light. With their placement under low, extended eaves, Wright also managed to preserve a sense of domestic privacy. With Heller House, Wright also employed the hidden entrance—a trademark of this and many subsequent designs—which he felt was more seemly and discreet than a front door fully exposed to the world. Take note of the friezes around the upper level of the house; if you visit Wright's home and studio in Oak Park, you'll see that he installed copies of them around the fireplace in his office.

Now return along Woodlawn Avenue to 1172 E. 55th St.:

6. **Woodlawn Tap.** If the University of Chicago had an equivalent of the Yale "Whiffenpoof Song," Woodlawn Tap would occupy the honored place of Mory's. Previously known as Jimmy's (for its longtime owner, who died in 1999), the bar is under new management and remains U. of C.'s main hangout. Indeed, it's the only tavern remaining from Hyde Park's golden era, before urban renewal obliterated a host of other gin mills that attracted the old college crowd. It's a traditional college bar, with a labyrinth of separate rooms, updated somewhat by the new owners. A few hard-core regulars hang along the bar; students fill the booths between classes, quaffing drafts and eating burgers.

Return one block east; just in from the corner at 55th Street is 5472 S. Kimbark Ave.:

7. **St. Thomas the Apostle Roman Catholic Church.** This house of worship gets a fair amount of attention from architecture buffs for two reasons. First, it doesn't look like a conventional Catholic church, but architect Francis Barry Byrne's 1924 design is highly regarded. Second, Byrne served an apprenticeship with Frank Lloyd Wright, and the influence of the Prairie School is evident in much that is unique about St. Thomas. The entryway in particular, a double curtain of delicate, highly ornamented terra-cotta, is definitely the Wright stuff— or, more accurately, reflects the influences of lyrical design that Wright picked up from his own svengali, Louis Sullivan.

As you head south along Kimbark and cross 55th Street, you are entering an area known as the:

8. **Golden Rectangle.** In Hyde Park, this is real estate heaven, a few blocks bordering the University of Chicago campus that contain the neighborhood's priciest and most desirable housing.

   Among the most elegant of these dwellings are several clusters of row houses down Kimbark Avenue. They wrap around 56th Street to the next block, Woodlawn, and are known as:

9. **Professor's Row.** In this group are 5558 S. Kimbark Ave. and 1220–1222, 1226, 1228, and 1234 E. 56th St. These homes were built collectively by several members of the university faculty; the brother of one was the chief architect. These houses look proper and staid, like gentlemen in morning suits attending a society wedding. Their landmark tile roofs, however, were the subject of a somewhat pedestrian controversy in recent years, when migrating parrots from South America selected them as a preferred nesting spot. Once the birds took up residence, they seemed to lose all further interest in returning south. Local wildlife partisans screamed "fowl" when the home-owners, allied with Illinois farmers who claimed the birds were a danger to crops, attempted to evict the intruders by force.

   At the corner of 56th and Woodlawn, turn back north to see:

10. **5537 S. Woodlawn Ave.** One of the great minds of modern nuclear science, Enrico Fermi, lived here with his family while working on the Manhattan Project and later as a member of the research faculty of the University of Chicago. Fermi received the 1938 Nobel Prize for physics; under the pretext of going to Stockholm to accept his prize, he and his family fled Italian fascism and settled in the United States. Fermilab, the Department of Energy's national laboratory in the western suburbs of Chicago, is named for him.

    During the next portion of our excursion, we will selectively tour the campus buildings of the:

11. **University of Chicago.** This brainy institution certainly doesn't rate on lists of top party schools. The U. of C. has a reputation for seriousness that surpasses virtually all other American institutions of higher learning. Just look at the list of faculty members, past and present, who've won the Nobel Prize—more than threescore, and the count seems to increase each year.

John D. Rockefeller, on behalf of the American Baptist Society, founded the university in 1890, on land donated and purchased from Chicago merchant prince Marshall Field. Given this trio of progenitors, it's no wonder that the university provided a haven for some of the most celebrated conservatives, such as Milton Friedman and Allan Bloom, to strut through the American academic scene in the 20th century. For the most part, however, it would not be fair to characterize the U. of C. as too liberal or too conservative. Few schools anywhere put a higher premium on getting to the truth that lies beyond the cant of competing ideologies. Here the Socratic method survives, embodied in the sentiments urged upon a recent class of incoming freshmen: "If someone asserts it, deny it; if someone denies it, assert it."

Henry Ives Cobb, a leading practitioner of the Romanesque Revival architecture still fashionable in the 1890s, was commissioned to provide a master plan in Gothic for the campus. The university trustees considered that style more suitable to an institution rooted in the more recent religious traditions of the West. Cobb rose to the occasion; he imagined two sets of quadrangles facing each other across a common green, where the buildings formed exterior ramparts, broken by gates and portals. The effect was not unlike that of a walled medieval monastery or, indeed, an English university. With some modification, this is essentially what the core of the campus came to resemble, making it one of the most idyllic settings for higher education in the country. Strolling the interior quads of this grand campus, one can be forgiven a pang of envy toward those privileged enough to study here.

On 56th Street, we'll delay entering the campus proper and walk a couple of blocks west to take in several of the newer buildings just north of this street and the main quads. At Greenwood Avenue, head north to our first stop, the:

12. **David and Alfred Smart Museum of Art.** The museum bears the names of its principal patrons, brothers who founded *Esquire* magazine. The museum's permanent collection contains more than 7,000 works ranging from classical antiquity to the contemporary. The curators' emphasis is on a program of frequently changing exhibitions around such intriguing themes as "Canceled: Exhibiting Experimental Art in China" and "Fear of Women in Late Nineteenth Century Art."

Outside the museum, the Vera and A. D. Elden Sculpture Garden leads to another significant arts institution, the:

13. **Court Theatre.** This attractively outfitted space affiliated with the university is used not by students but by a professional theater company. It stages well-regarded productions of works by Molière, Shakespeare, and other luminaries.

Now return to 56th Street and walk south on Ellis Avenue, toward the main campus. On the left (east) side of the street, about a third of the way down the block, look for:

14. *Nuclear Energy.* This 1967 abstract sculpture by Henry Moore marks the spot where the world's first controlled nuclear chain reaction occurred on December 2, 1942. Enrico Fermi headed the team that accomplished the historic feat with an atomic pile installed in a squash court under what was then Stagg Stadium. Today, a new, massive complex dominates this site. It's the:

15. **Joseph Regenstein Library.** The architect for this act of "concrete brutalism," as one of his critics uncharitably characterized the design, was Walter A. Netsch, Jr., whose home is mentioned in Walking Tour 6, "Old Town." Netsch's other major commission in the city, the University of Illinois at Chicago, a bit south and west of

the Loop, is also much denigrated by critics and, it seems, not well loved by the public either. One never hears a good word about this campus of concrete slabs, the model for which seems to have been that South American moonscape, Brasília, the prefab capital of Brazil. To say that the Regenstein Library clashes with practically every other campus building would not be an overstatement—or get much argument from U. of C. alumni.

From here, the architectural landscape soars to a higher plane, one unabashedly traditional in every respect. The campus radiates an atmosphere of other-worldliness and well-being that is completely appropriate to the work of scholarship. Across from the library, enter the main campus on 57th Street, between Ellis and University avenues, by way of a structure that may look familiar to those who recall the opening scene of the 1989 film *When Harry Met Sally* (it's when Harry first met Sally):

16. **Cobb Gate.** The intricately carved gate, with the inscription "Hull Laboratories," was designed and constructed by Henry Ives Cobb in 1901, soon before he was replaced as campus architect. This work demonstrated his commitment to the Gothic detailing, with which he adorned practically every building whose construction he supervised, before budget cutbacks put an end to expensive decoration. The "grotesques," the mythic figures climbing to the tip of the gate's pointed gable, have come to represent an allegory of undergraduate progress. According to one account in a University of Chicago publication, "The largest figures, at the base of the eaves on either side, are said to be the admissions counselor and college examiner defying ready passage. Above them are the first-year college students with tenuous academic grip, about to lose their footing. The second-year students, with firmer grasp and heads erect, scurry ahead. Snarling at the second-year students to keep them at a respectful distance, the third-year students strain to reach the top. The fourth-year students, having mastered the slippery slope, stand proudly at the educational pinnacle."

Past the gate and immediately to your left is a loggia, a roofed arcade or passageway. Cross through it to:

17. **Hutchinson Court.** An English sunken garden provides the model for this stone-paved courtyard, the site of formal receptions, recitals, student gatherings, and outdoor performances. The designer was John Olmsted, son of Frederick Law Olmsted, the great landscape architect who came to Chicago to supervise the redesign of Jackson Park for the World's Columbian Exposition.

    Enclosing Hutchinson Court is a group of connected buildings known as the Tower Group. Mitchell Tower, which anchors this corner of the quad, was inspired by a similar bell tower at Magdalen College at Oxford University in England. The tower contains the Palmer chimes, named for the university's first woman dean and installed in 1908. They are used in the ancient English art of change ringing, in which the bells are rung in every possible order and permutation, creating a din that is not universally applauded by residents, on campus or off.

    Take a Break You may wish to stop at a newly refurbished cafe called the **C-Shop,** offering all the usual suspects—pastries, ice cream, and gourmet coffee—in a suitably collegiate setting.

    Walk out the cafe doors into the building, then walk left and you'll come to:

18. **Hutchinson Commons.** The spirit of the British public school is alive and well inside this former men's dining hall, a 115-foot-long but relatively narrow room. The cathedral-high, hammer-beamed ceiling, raised oak-paneled walls, arched and leaded windows, and over-sized fireplaces contribute to an unmistakably British atmosphere of a bygone era. Hutchinson Commons makes an anachronistic seating for a cafeteria, open to all.

    Directly across the entrance to Hutchinson Commons is the:

19. **Reynolds Clubhouse.** Also built originally for male students, the Reynolds Clubhouse once contained rooms for recreational activities like billiards and bowling, as well as a library and reading room. Echoes of historicism dominate the architecture of this building, the grand central

staircase in the entrance hall suggesting something of the traditional English manor house. Today Reynolds Clubhouse serves as a union for the entire student body. It holds Mandel Hall, a handsome auditorium used for concerts, lectures, and other performances, and a second-floor lounge with pool tables, air hockey, TVs, and concessions. Relax a few minutes in the McCormick Tribune Lounge's plush armchairs if you need a rest.

Return to the courtyard facing Cobb Gate. That ornamental pool of water next to the Erman Biology Center is called:

20. **Botany Pond.** This is also the landscaping work of John Olmsted; the science faculty guided him when the pond was originally stocked with exotic specimens and plants from the botany department. Today, the pond is used for experiments in ecology. Take a moment to enjoy the enormous ginkgo tree.

Now continue on to the central rectangle between the two quads (basically the area where you see a traffic circle) and walk to the right (west), passing between two buildings and crossing Ellis Avenue to the:

21. **University Bookstore.** This many-gabled red-brick building dates from 1902; John D. Rockefeller funded the project specifically to house the University of Chicago Press. Since 1971, the building has housed the University Bookstore, which sells durable sportswear in addition to many textbooks and trade books. The bookstore is closed on Sunday.

Now, cross Ellis Avenue again and re-enter the quadrangle, walking right (south) toward the first building in the South Quad:

22. **Cobb Lecture Hall** (no. 5811). On October 1, 1892, when the university received its first class of students, Cobb Hall was the University of Chicago. The first of 18 buildings designed by Henry Ives Cobb, it's named for the unrelated donor of the building, Silas B. Cobb. In the early days, each department occupying the second to fourth floors of Cobb Hall had its own classrooms and library. A massive renovation, begun in 1963, gutted and

transformed the interior of the voluminous structure. The project scrupulously retained every detail of Cobb Hall's distinctive Gothic exterior. Inside, a worthy diversion is the Renaissance Society, which despite its name is a forward-looking contemporary art gallery. Founded in 1915, the society was one of the first institutions to introduce Chicagoans to the likes of major figures like Picasso, Miró, Alexander Calder, and Cindy Sherman. Directly opposite Cobb Hall's main entrance is the "C" bench, a gift of the class of 1903; until the 1960s, only varsity lettermen and their dates could sit there.

Across the courtyard from Cobb Hall is Swift Hall, the divinity school. Connected to this building in a separate wing by way of a cloister is the:

23. **Joseph Bond Chapel.** Even the nonbeliever and the iconoclast will shudder in awe and approval when seeing the interior of this inspired showcase of ecclesiastical craftsmanship, which dates from 1926. It's hard to imagine a chapel being more richly or lovingly decorated. Charting a course for the architects and other contributors, a professor of the New Testament from the University divinity school ensured that the gospels' messages would be fully manifest on every available space. They're etched in both the woodwork and the stained-glass windows. Divine perorations are scrolled across the top of the entrance, while the beatitudes are carved into a frieze above the interior wainscoting. Every niche has its carved figure or form, whether a dove with an olive branch, an angel blowing its horn, or a cluster of allegorical grapes. The leaded windows are a masterpiece of intricacy and grace. The Bond Chapel, with a seating capacity of 300, is diminutive but not tiny, and is a community favorite for weddings and memorial services.

Follow the roadway running through the center of the campus (noting the castle-like Harper Memorial Library on your right) to 5757 S. University Ave., where you'll find a red-brick and stone Gothic-towered building, the:

24. **Chicago Theological Seminary.** This double-winged complex, an independent institution not connected to the university, holds two points of interest: the well-stocked

subterranean Seminary Co-op Bookstore, and the tiny, jewel-like Hilton Memorial Chapel.

Across 58th Street from the seminary is a renowned archeological repository, the:

25. **Oriental Institute.** Carvings on the bas-reliefs around the main entrance at 1155 E. 58th St. depict the meeting of the East, symbolized by a lion, and the West, represented by a bison. The great historical figures and monuments of each civilization are also juxtaposed. From the East, they are the pyramids, the Sphinx, the ruins of Peresopolis, along with Hammurabi of Babylon (the lawgiver), Darius of Persia, and Thutmose III of Egypt. From the West are Notre-Dame and the Parthenon, as well as Herodotus, Alexander, and Caesar. But don't stand at the doorway; take a few minutes to peruse the extraordinary collection of antiquities inside. How often do you have a chance to see finds from many world digs, some of which date from as far back as 9000 B.C., all in one place?

    Note: Much of the museum has been closed for a major renovation and expansion. The Egyptian and Persian galleries have reopened with entirely new installations. The Institute's gift shop, the Suq, which carries fine and unusual imported crafts and jewelry from the Middle East, remains open during construction.

    Walking along 58th Street, go to the corner of Woodlawn Avenue and turn right. Half a block to the south (essentially behind the Oriental Institute) is the magnificent:

26. **Rockefeller Memorial Chapel.** Folks, this is no chapel; by any measure or account, the building, raised between 1925 and 1928, is a full-blown church, if not an actual cathedral. The dimensions are imposing: 265 feet long and 120 feet wide. The height from sidewalk to roofline is 102 feet. The entrance faces 59th Street. Once the chapel stood open 24 hours a day, but the university president gave this explanation for the decision to close it overnight: "Unfortunately, more souls have been conceived at Rockefeller Chapel than have been saved there."

    This news may or may not have pleased the chapel's architect, Bertram Grosvenor Goodhue, whose name sounds Puritanical. But Goodhue, as a leading proponent of the Gothic Revival and of the Arts and Crafts movement, was clearly an aesthetic sensualist. The Arts and Crafts movement began in Europe in the mid–19th century as a reaction to mass production and promoted the decorative arts and a return to fine craftsmanship. As for the Gothic content of the chapel's design, Goodhue did not borrow from a single or even a set of existing models; he began by reinterpreting Gothic architecture according to its first principles, which he had studied assiduously.

Through his commitment to authenticity, Goodhue managed to achieve a degree of originality that created a sense of novelty, extending to the building's unusual proportions, its irregular shape, and the placement of the massive tower over the eastern transept. Construction techniques were also rigidly traditional: The building is solid masonry, faced with Indiana limestone; arches and buttresses are actually load-bearing, not decorative, and provide true structural support. The walls of the tower are 8 feet thick.

The chapel is decorated elaborately, both inside and out. The numerous carvings, sculptures, and inscriptions provide a world view of religion, politics, history, and philosophy. Among the more than 70 statues decorating the exterior walls are 15 life-sized figures of the world's most revered thinkers and holy men placed among the turrets and gable of the south facade. They include Abraham, Moses, Zoroaster, Plato, John the Baptist, Francis of Assisi, Luther, and Calvin, with Jesus at the apex. Even Jan Hus, the great pre-Reformation martyr who inspired many nondoctrinal Christian sects, like the American Baptists, is there (on the west column alongside the window). Look for a figure of the chapel architect, cradling a model of the building in his arms, to the right of the doorway off Woodlawn.

There is so much more to see on the outside that you will need a university guidebook to take it all in. The same applies to the many details inside the chapel. Here we can highlight only a handful of the interior delights: the unique glazed-tile ceiling 80 feet above you, the masterfully carved organ screen in the rear of the chapel, and, above all, the dazzling symphony of stained glass above the altar. Your attention will return to the stained glass more than once, involuntarily, so powerful is the force and concentration of the light.

Return now to the intersection of Woodlawn Avenue and 58th Street. Cross to the northeast corner, where you will see the:

27. **Frederick C. Robie House.** Wright designed Robie House in 1906 for a man who manufactured motorcycles and bicycles. Many experts consider Robie House Frank Lloyd Wright's supreme achievement in domestic architecture. But the cold manner in which the critics dissect the elements of this dwelling, seen as a perfect abstraction of Wright's classic "Prairie House," is a key to my somewhat heretical opinion that Robie House was perhaps never a very "livable" space.

Robie House lacks the warmth Wright achieved with so many of his other Prairie School homes, not least his own Oak Park cottage (which only evolved into an example of that genre over the years as Wright's mastery of the idiom developed). With Robie House, Wright had basically arrived at the end of his Prairie School experimentation. The Robie family lived here for only 2½ years, and by 1926 the house was empty.

For years thereafter, Robie House kicked around in the university system as an annex for classrooms, dormitory space, and even a refectory. It was scheduled for demolition in 1957; only a last-ditch effort by a group of preservation-minded individuals saved it from the wrecker's ball. Today the home is in the middle of an extensive 10-year restoration, inside and out, and is managed by Oak Park's Frank Lloyd Wright Home and Studio Foundation. When touring Robie House, consider that its intrinsic appeal is less that of a plausible domestic shelter and more that of an artist's exquisite model, a culmination in the abstract of the great architect's vision at a point when that vision was about to undergo a major transformation. If you missed out on a tour, you can still take a peek: Facing the bookstore, which is in the building's attached garage, walk to the left until you reach the stairs leading to the porch and a glimpse into the home.

With your back to the house, turn left, following 58th Street east to Blackstone Avenue. Turn right toward the:

28. **Midway Plaisance.** Frederick Law Olmsted laid out this elongated green during the construction of the World's Columbian Exposition to link Jackson and Washington parks, at opposite ends of the original Hyde Park village boundaries. The Exposition's entertainment zone, centered around the world's first Ferris wheel, was here, and the term "the midway" came to be associated with carnivals and amusement parks everywhere.

Continue 1 block east (left). Before you reach the railroad crossing, turn left on Harper Avenue. Here, between 59th and 57th streets, are remnants of Hyde Park's first planned community:

29. **Rosalie Villas.** A developer named Rosalie Buckingham purchased this land in 1883, with plans for a subdivision of 42 houses on spacious lots to create a semirural environment. She hired George Pullman's architect, Solon S. Berman, who had recently completed the building of the Pullman planned community to the south. Many of the cottages Berman and his colleagues constructed remain, in various states of repair, and line both sides of the block; their eclectic color schemes and overgrown gardens give the street a distinctively countercultural flavor.

At 57th Street walk east, passing a couple of used book shops and a cafe, and cross Lake Park Avenue before you enter:

30. **Jackson Park.** When laid out in 1871 by Olmsted and Vaux, the team that designed Central Park in New York City, this was known as South Park. The full plan for the park was not carried out until 1895, after Olmsted had returned to Chicago with his sons to help mount the World's Columbian Exposition. A short walk beyond the point where we entered Jackson Park is the final stop on our tour of Hyde Park:

31. **The Museum of Science and Industry,** the only major structure that survived the Exposition. Today, the world-famous museum boasts more than 2,000 exhibits spread over 14 acres, including a full-scale replica of a

coal mine, an original World War II German U-Boat submarine, and a United Airlines 727. Given the massive number of exhibits and vast amount of space the museum covers, you should probably schedule at least half a day for a visit here. The museum is open weekdays 9am to 5pm and weekends 9:30am to 5:30pm. It is closed on Thanksgiving. Admission is free on Thursdays.

Essentials

Only by walking its streets can you savor the real spice of Chicago. You cannot truly claim to know a city that you haven't crisscrossed by foot. Chicago is fertile ground for long excursions: Skyscrapers give way to green spaces, which in turn yield to industrial wastelands and riverscapes (the Chicago River seems to be everywhere). Let this guide be your introduction to discovering Chicago by foot. Obviously, you can't wander off just anywhere. Use your own instincts and information from your hotel staff and the tourist office to set realistic boundaries.

ORIENTATION/CITY LAYOUT

Chicago's streets follow a grid system. The city's somewhat stubby, elongated dimensions make the resulting shape irregular, but the graphic pattern remains. The great exceptions are the city's half dozen or so major diagonal thoroughfares (which are said to follow old Native American trails) and the interconnected network of freeways.

Street numbering does not originate at the city's geographical midpoint, but nearer to its historic and commercial center, more north than south, and so far east as almost to border Lake Michigan.

FINDING AN ADDRESS   Point zero is the downtown intersection of State and Madison streets; State divides east and west addresses and Madison divides north and south addresses. From here, Chicago's highly predictable addressing system begins. Using the grid, it is relatively easy to plot the distance in miles between any two points in the city.

Addresses on virtually all of Chicago's principal north-south and east-west arteries proceed by increments of 400 per block, regardless of the number of smaller streets between them. And each difference of 400 numbers in an address is equivalent to half a mile. Starting at Madison Street (point zero) and traveling north along State Street for 1 mile, you will come to 800 N. State St., which intersects Chicago Avenue. Continue uptown for another half mile and you arrive at the 1200 block of North State Street at Division Street. And so it goes right to the city line, with suburban Evanston at the 7600 block north, 9½ miles from this arbitrary center.

The same rule applies when traveling south, or east to west. Heading west from State Street along Madison, Halsted Street—at 800 West Madison—is a mile's distance; Racine, at the 1200 block of West Madison, is 1½ miles from the center. Madison then continues westward to Chicago's boundary along Austin Avenue with the suburb of Oak Park, which at 6000 West Madison Street is approximately 7½ miles from point zero.

The side of any square formed by the principal avenues (noted in dark or red ink on most maps) represents half a mile in any direction. Understanding how Chicago's grid system works is particularly important to visitors who wish to walk a lot in the city's many neighborhoods and who want to calculate distances in advance.

GETTING AROUND

By Public Transportation

The Chicago Transit Authority (CTA) operates an extensive system of trains and buses throughout the city. The sturdy system carries more than 1.5 million passengers a day. Subways and elevated trains (the El) are generally safe and reliable, though it's advisable to avoid long rides through unfamiliar neighborhoods late at night.

The Metra commuter trains and PACE buses operate between the city and surrounding suburbs.

Chicago Orientation

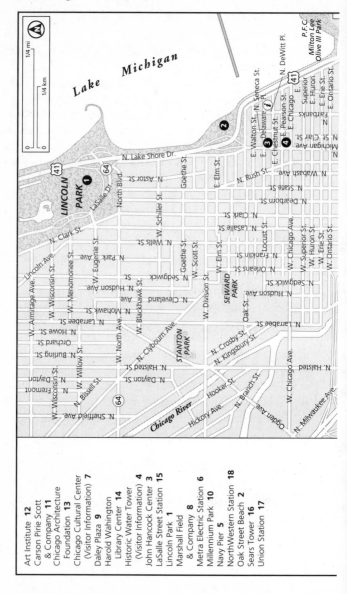

CTA INFORMATION The CTA operates a telephone information service (☎ **836-7000,** TTY 836-4949 from any area code in the city or suburbs; www.transitchicago.com) daily from 5am to 1am. Call to ask how to get from where you are

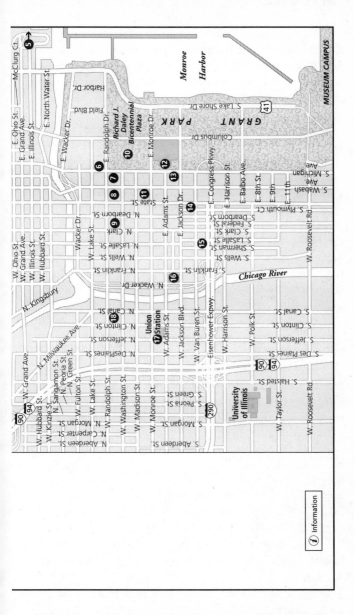

to where you need to go. Make sure you specify your requirements—for example, the fastest route, the simplest (the route with the fewest transfers or least amount of walking), and so forth. You also can look up route information on the Web.

The CTA has adopted a farecard system that automatically deducts fares from a plastic card. Each bus or El ride costs $1.50, no matter how far you travel. You can buy a reusable farecard with a preset value already stored, or you can obtain a card at vending machines at all CTA train stations and charge them with the amount you choose. The turnstiles at the El stations and the fare boxes on buses automatically deduct the cost of a transfer (30¢); you're permitted two additional transfers within two hours. Although buses do accept farecards, you can't buy a farecard on the bus; either pick one up at an El station first, or pay with exact change when you board. The same card can be recharged repeatedly.

Out-of-towners may find it economical to buy a Visitor's Pass, which works like a farecard 7 and allows individual users unlimited rides on the El and CTA buses over a 24-hour period for $5. Hotels, museums, transportation hubs, and Chicago Office of Tourism visitor information centers sell the passes.

An excellent comprehensive CTA map and route maps for specific lines are available at most subway or El fare booths, or by calling ☎ **312/836-7000.**

While some CTA stations and many CTA buses are fully accessible to passengers with disabilities, the agency also provides door-to-door service to qualified users. Call the CTA's paratransit services at ☎ **312/432-7025** or TTY 312/432-7116.

BY THE EL & THE SUBWAY   The Rapid Transit system operates five major lines: Red (north-south), Green (west-south), Blue (west-northwest to O'Hare Airport), Brown (a zigzag northern route also known as the Ravenswood), and Orange (southwest to Midway Airport). The express Purple Line serves Evanston; a smaller Yellow Line in Skokie links to the north-south Red Line. Skokie and Evanston are suburbs on Chicago's northern boundary.

See the inside back cover for a map of the Chicago transit system.

Study your CTA map carefully before boarding any train. Most trains run around the clock, with service less frequent in off-peak and overnight hours. Some stations that serve the suburbs close after work hours (as early as 8:30pm) and remain closed on Saturday, Sunday, and holidays.

BY BUS Virtually every destination in the city lies within a short walk from a bus stop. Other than on foot, the best way to get around Chicago's warren of neighborhoods—and the best way to see what's around you—is by riding a public bus. (The view from the elevated trains can be pretty dramatic, too. The difference is that on the trains you get the backyards, while on the bus you see the buildings' facades and the street life.)

PACE buses (☎ **836-7000** from any city area code, TTY 836-4949; www.pacebus.com) serve the suburbs. They run every 20 to 30 minutes during rush hour, operating until mid-evening Monday to Friday, and early evening on weekends. Numbers 208 and above designate suburban bus routes. Few lines have marked stops, and vehicles may be flagged down at intersections. Information is available on the Internet. For information about paratransit services, call ☎ **847/364-7223** or TTY 847/364-5093.

BY TROLLEY Free rubber-wheeled trolleys (not to be confused with paid tourist trolleys) link many of the city's major cultural and entertainment sites. Routes operate throughout the Loop and the Magnificent Mile: to and from Navy Pier, with stops along Grand Avenue and Illinois Street; along Michigan Avenue from the Museum Campus to Water Tower Park; and from the Loop to Chinatown. Trolley routes serve many CTA and Metra stations. Look for brown signs identifying trolley stops. Schedules vary by season; for more information, call ☎ **877/244-2246.**

BY TRAIN The Metra commuter railroad (☎ **312/322-6777,** TTY 312/322-6774 weekdays; at other times 312/836-7000, TTY 312/836-4949; www.metrarail.com), which serves the suburbs, has terminals at several downtown locations. They include Union Station, at Adams and Canal; LaSalle Street Station, at LaSalle and Van Buren; the Northwestern Station, at Madison and Canal; and Randolph Street Station, at Randolph and Michigan Avenue. The Metra Electric runs along Lake Michigan to Hyde Park. Commuter trains have graduated fare schedules based on the distance you ride.

By Taxi

Taxis are very affordable for short runs—for moving around the downtown area, for example, or for excursions to the Near North Side neighborhoods of Old Town and Lincoln Park, or to Wicker Park on the Near West Side. Even budget-conscious travelers will find taxis a viable option for short runs. Beyond that, as in any large city, a cab ride is not economical.

Some cab companies are **Checker** (☎ **312/CHECKER** or 312/243-2537), **Yellow** (☎ **312/TAXI-CAB** or 312/829-4222), and **Flash** (☎ 773/561-1444).

By Car

Chicago's layout is so logical that even for a stranger, driving around the city is a relatively easy task. On the whole, traffic seems to run fairly smoothly at most times of the day. Rush-hour traffic jams, however, are as daunting in Chicago as in other U.S. cities. However, the combination of wide streets and strategically spaced expressways running in all directions makes for generally easy riding.

The great diagonal corridors violate the grid pattern at key points in the city and shorten many a trip that would otherwise be tedious on the checkerboard surface of Chicago streets. Lake Shore Drive (also known as the Outer Dr.) is one of the most scenic and useful urban thoroughfares anywhere. You can travel the length of the city (and beyond) never far from the great sea-lake that is certainly Chicago's most awesome natural feature.

RENTALS   Chicago has outlets of the "big four" car-rental companies: **Avis** (☎ **800/831-2847**), **Budget** (☎ **800/527-0700**), **Hertz** (☎ **800/654-3131**), and **National** (☎ **800/227-7368**).

DRIVING RULES   One bizarre anomaly is the absence of signal lights off the principal avenues. One block east or west of the Magnificent Mile (N. Michigan Ave.)—one of the most traveled streets in the city—only stop signs control the flow of traffic. Once you've become accustomed to the system, it works smoothly, with pedestrians and motorists alike advancing in their proper turn. A right turn on red is allowed unless otherwise posted.

PARKING Parking regulations are vigorously enforced throughout the city of Chicago. There are few urban experiences more discouraging than having to retrieve your impounded car from the police tow-away lot. To avoid it, be sure to check parking signs at curbside, or find a parking lot and pay the premium prices you would in any metropolitan area.

The most affordable downtown parking is the city-run lot at **Grant Park** (☎ **312/747-2519**); entrances are at Michigan at Van Buren (south garage) and Michigan at Monroe (north garage). Private parking lots, which are scattered throughout the Loop and Magnificent Mile, include **Midcontinental Plaza Garage,** 55 E. Monroe St. (☎ **312/986-6821**); and **Navy Pier Parking,** 600 E. Grand Ave. (☎ **312/595-7437**); prepare for sticker shock, though, when you see your bill.

By Boat

Wendella Commuter Boats (☎ **312/337-1446;** www. wendellaboats.com) operates a river taxi that ferries passengers from a dock on the northwest side of the Michigan Avenue Bridge (by the Wrigley Building) to a dock at Madison Street, near the Metra train station and the Sears Tower. The ride each way takes about 8 minutes and is popular with both visitors and commuters. The service operates from April to October, every 10 minutes from 7am to 7pm. The ride costs $2 each way, $3 round trip. Wendella also operates service from the Michigan Avenue Bridge to the River East dock in the Streeterville neighborhood.

Shoreline Sightseeing (☎ **312/222-9328;** www.shore linesightseeing.com) carries passengers on the lake between Navy Pier and the Museum Campus and on the Chicago River between Navy Pier and the Sears Tower (Adams St. and the river). The water taxis operate daily 10am to 6pm between Memorial Day and Labor Day; they cost $6 for adults, $5 for seniors, $3 for children.

FAST FACTS Chicago

American Express Travel service offices are downtown at 122 S. Michigan Ave. (☎ **312/435-2595**); on the Magnificent

Mile at 605 N. Michigan Ave. (☎ 312/435-2570); and in Lincoln Park at 2338 N. Clark (☎ 773/477-4000).

Area Code   Area codes within the city limits are 312 (downtown and core neighborhoods) and 773 (rest of the city); suburban area codes are 708, 847, 630, and 815.

Bookstores   The big chain bookstores have a major presence in Chicago. The many excellent independent shops include **Brent Books & Cards,** downtown at 309 W. Washington St. (☎ 312/364-0126); **Barbara's Bookstore,** in Old Town at 1350 N. Wells St. (☎ 312/642-5044); **Unabridged Books,** in Lakeview at 3251 N. Broadway (☎ 773/883-9119); and **Seminary Co-op Bookstore,** in Hyde Park at 5757 S. University Ave. (☎ 773/752-4381).

Business Hours   Shops generally open around 10am and close by 7pm Monday to Saturday. Most stores stay open late at least one evening a week. Certain businesses, like bookstores, are almost always open in the evening all week. Many shops are open on Sunday as well, usually for the afternoon. Malls, like Water Tower Place at 835 N. Michigan Ave., are generally open until 7pm and are open Sunday.

Banking hours in Chicago are normally from 9am (8am in some cases) to 5pm Monday to Friday. Some banks remain open later on some afternoons and evenings.

Climate   Chicago has a four-season climate, with extremes of cold and heat. The average high temperature in January, generally the coldest month, is 20°F (-6°C); in July and August, the hottest months, the average high temperature is 84°F (29°C).

Emergencies   Dial ☎ **911** for a city ambulance.

Media   The *Chicago Tribune* and the *Chicago Sun-Times* are the two major daily newspapers. The *Chicago Reader,* an excellent free weekly, prints articles of local interest and all current entertainment and cultural listings. The monthly *Chicago* magazine is a good source for restaurant reviews. On the Web, a couple of useful sites are www.metromix.com and www.chicago.citysearch.com.

Restrooms   Fast-food outlets are always a good bet for clean restrooms, as are hotel lobbies. There are public restrooms near

Buckingham Fountain in Grant Park and in park facilities along the lakefront.

Safety Whenever you're traveling in an unfamiliar city or country, stay alert. Wear a money belt, and don't sling your camera or purse over your shoulder. This will minimize the possibility of you becoming a victim of crime. Every society has its criminals. It's your responsibility to be aware and be alert even in the most heavily touristed areas. In Chicago, be careful of where you walk alone at night. Consult your hotel concierge or staff or a local resident if in doubt.

Taxes The local sales tax is 8.75%; the hotel tax is 14.9%.

Tourist Information The **Chicago Office of Tourism** (☎ **312/744-2400,** TTY 312/744-2947; www.ci.chi.il. us/Tourism). The **Illinois Bureau of Tourism** (☎ **800/ 2CONNECT,** TTY 800/406-6418; www.enjoyillinois.com).

There are visitor information centers at the **Chicago Cultural Center,** 77 E. Randolph St. at Michigan Avenue (open weekdays 10am–6pm, Sat 10am–5pm, Sun 11am– 5pm), and the **Chicago Water Works,** 163 E. Pearson St. at North Michigan (open daily 7:30am–7pm). The **Illinois Market Place** gift shop at Navy Pier, 600 E. Grand Ave., distributes brochures and other information.

Useful Telephone Numbers For directory assistance, dial ☎ **411.** For the time, dial ☎ **312/976-1616** and for the **weather forecast,** dial ☎ **312/976-1212** (you will be charged a fee for these services). For **movie showtimes,** call 312/444-FILM.

Index

Wickedly honest guides for sophisticated travelers—and those who want to be.

Irreverent Guide to Amsterdam
Irreverent Guide to Boston
Irreverent Guide to Chicago
Irreverent Guide to Las Vegas
Irreverent Guide to London
Irreverent Guide to Los Angeles
Irreverent Guide to Manhattan
Irreverent Guide to New Orleans
Irreverent Guide to Paris
Irreverent Guide to Rome
Irreverent Guide to San Francisco
Irreverent Guide to Seattle & Portland
Irreverent Guide to Vancouver
Irreverent Guide to Walt Disney World®
Irreverent Guide to Washington, D.C.

Available at bookstores everywhere.

Booked seat 6A, open return.

Rented red 4-wheel drive.

Reserved cabin, no running water.

Discovered space.

With over 700 airlines, 50,000 hotels, 50 rental car companies and 5,000 cruise and vacation packages, you can create the perfect getaway for you. Choose the car, the room, even the ground you walk on.

Travelocity.com
A Sabre Company
Go Virtually Anywhere.

You Need
A Vacation.

700 Airlines, 50,000 Hotels, 50 Rental Car
Companies, And A Million Ways To Save Money.

Travelocity.com
A Sabre Company
Go Virtually Anywhere.